CREATIVE IDEAS
FOR
CHRISTMAS
1 9 8 5

COMPILED AND EDITED BY NANCY JANICE FITZPATRICK

Oxmoor House®

Library of Congress Catalog Card Number: 84-063033

ISBN: O-8487-0648-X

Manufactured in the United States of America
First Printing

Executive Editor: Candace Conard Bromberg
Production Manager: Jerry Higdon
Art Director: Bob Nance

Creative Ideas for Christmas 1985

Senior Editor: Nancy Janice Fitzpatrick
Editor: Kathleen English
Assistant Editor: Alison Nichols
Foods Editor: Debby Maugans Barton
Editorial Assistant: Pamela Hall
Photography Stylists: Beverly Morrow, Lisa Gant,
  Susann Hodges
Pattern Artist: Don K. Smith
Copy Chief: Mary Jean Haddin
Designers: Viola Andrycich, Diana Smith Morrison

CONTENTS

INTRODUCTION

WELCOME THE SEASON 1

YOUR CHRISTMAS KITCHEN...................92

INTRODUCTION

Christmas. Say it out loud, and it has a fresh and thrilling ring to it, like tinkling bells, singing voices, or—whisper it now—footfalls on the snow. Christmas. The very thought of it can bring a smile—the kind that starts in the corners of your mouth and rushes to warm your heart and soul.

That is what this book is about—smiles and Christmas. We want to bring you both. With ideas and instructions for holiday decorating, gift-giving, and entertaining, we hope to take the guesswork out of your handmade Christmas projects, so that you can confidently create those personal touches that loved ones will cherish. And as you work, smile in anticipation of the answering smiles that your thoughtful labors will inspire.

WELCOME THE SEASON

Holiday decorations—angels or elves, twinkling lights or pungent pine garlands—embody the joy and wonder of the season. And whether arranging old favorites or making new ones, decorating for the happy days ahead stirs excitement and heightens anticipation. To deck your halls, choose from the diverse and lively collection of ideas pictured on the following pages.

TWINKLING HEARTS
IN PUNCHED TIN

Illuminate your holiday decorations with golden candlelight flickering through perforated designs in tin. Heart-shaped shadows slanting across walls will deliver a romantic nighttime mood.

A country heart pattern guides your awl for punching buckets and cups; then florist's clay snugs candles in place. Flourishes of greenery and ribbon tie these novel lanterns to the rest of your Christmas decor.

YOU WILL NEED:
patterns on page 124
tin cups and buckets (with soldered
   seams)
tape
4″ awl
hammer
florist's clay
candles
greenery and ribbons (optional)

To support surface of tin for punching, fill cups and buckets with water and freeze. To help prevent buckling of the containers' bottoms, freeze just ½″ water first, then add more water and freeze the remainder.

Prepare a waterproof working surface by laying a towel over plastic. Transfer patterns to paper and tape to containers.

To punch, place awl on each dot and hit with the hammer. For uniform holes, hit only one time and use consistent force. (If you must interrupt process, remove ice and fit a plastic bag inside the container. Fill bag with water, and refreeze.)

When all dots have been punched, remove the pattern gradually, checking for missed sections. When finished, rinse out remaining ice and dry container. (If bottom has buckled, hammer flat.)

Tape florist's clay to bottoms of containers and insert candles in clay. Add greenery and ribbon if desired.

A CHRISTMAS GOOSE MAKES A MERRY MAILBOX

Collect Christmas cards and compliments while extending season's greetings, with this handsome goose mailbox cover. Previous woodworking experience would be helpful, although the dedicated beginner will find this within his or her ability.

A bow or wreath around the goose neck conceals nails and completes the festive look!

YOU WILL NEED (for standard size mailbox):
17 (1½" x 28") ¼" wooden slats
5 ft. (1" x 12") wood
band saw
C clamps
1 (9" x 13") piece ½" plywood
drill with ¼" bit
wood glue
nails
2 (¼" x 2") wood screws
hammer
rasp (a wood-cutting file to shape goose head)
sandpaper
black and gray spray paint
red and white acrylic paint

From the 1" x 12" wood, cut the following pieces:

3 (7½" x 12") pieces for goose head—length on grain of wood

2 (9" x 10") pieces for end pieces

For goose head, apply glue to 1 entire surface of 2 of the 7½" x 12" pieces and stack the 3 pieces. Clamp with C clamps and let dry. Trace the flag on your mailbox. Transfer flag pattern to the plywood, and cut out. Sand flag, and drill a ¼" hole in staff.

Trace the end of your mailbox, and add 1¼" to all sides. Cut the rear end piece from a 9" x 10" piece of wood. For the front end piece, glue the other 9" x 10" piece to the plywood piece, trim excess plywood, and clamp with C clamps. After glue has dried, cut to same size as rear end piece. To allow for opening the mailbox door, make a

pattern by tracing the door and adding ¼" to top and sides. Center and transfer to front end piece. Begin at bottom edge and cut an arch.

To assemble the body frame, measure length of mailbox, and position front end piece (plywood side facing rear) and rear end piece that distance apart. Nail slats around front end piece flush with front edge. Then nail slats to rear end piece. (Slats will extend several inches beyond edge.)

Remove the C clamps from the three 7½" x 12" pieces. Using photograph and Figure as a guide, sketch goose head onto wood, and use band saw to cut out. Round edges of head with rasp and sand smooth. Place head on body frame and nail from the underside to secure.

To shape goose tail, measure 7" from rear end piece along bottom slat. Draw a diagonal line from this point to the top corner of the sixth slat above, and saw along this line. Repeat for other side.

Spray-paint body gray and head black. With white acrylic paint, add eyes, and neck and feather details, according to photo. Paint top portion of flag red and staff gray. To attach flag, drill hole near front edge of fourth slat from bottom of frame and insert a wood screw through flag into frame. Insert a second wood screw into frame 4" up from flag base, to hold flag in place when not in use. If desired, place a small wreath or ribbon around goose neck.

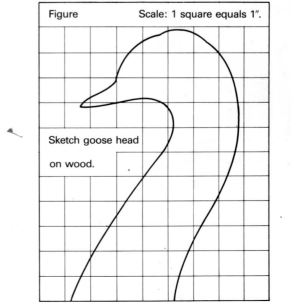

Figure   Scale: 1 square equals 1".

Sketch goose head on wood.

'TWAS THE NIGHT BEFORE CHRISTMAS

Designs can often be translated in a variety of ways—by using different materials, techniques, or a larger or smaller scale. The cheery holiday wall hanging shown here is one of those designs. This canvas decoration can be made in a twinkling, because it is primarily painted by stenciling, a technique that allows fast application of repeating designs. The Santa figure is outlined with markers, and then solid areas are painted with a brush. Shading is added with markers.

Patterns for each of the individual areas of the design—Saint Nick, the reindeer, houses and trees, and moon and stars—may be used for matching decorations. For instance, the star and moon patterns that form the corner squares of the hanging were used to make stamps for quick holiday impressions on wrapping paper, cards, or fabric.

On the following pages are two more decorations derived from the wall hanging motifs—wooden cutouts made from the reindeer, and the house and tree patterns. Use your ingenuity to apply these motifs to your favorite craft mediums.

STAMPED ORNAMENTS:
patterns on page 127
Dr. Scholl's self-adhesive foot pad
wood block (scrap)
craft knife
lightweight canvas
acrylic paints
aluminum pie tin
newspaper
ribbon (for hangers)

Transfer pattern to foot pad and to wood block. (You can use stencil from wall hanging as a template.) Cut the design out of the pad. Remove backing and attach to corresponding area on wood block.

Iron canvas, mark 4" squares for ornaments and spread on a flat, protected surface. Pour paint just to cover bottom of pie tin. To transfer the design, dip stamp in paint, blot on newspaper if necessary, and place in the center of each fabric square.

Cut out the squares, and with right sides facing, sew 2 squares together on 3 sides. Turn right sides out, stuff, and slip-stitch opening closed. Tack on ribbon hangers.

STENCILED SANTA WALL HANGING:
patterns on page 126
38" x 45½" piece of canvas
clear acetate sheet (for stencils)
masking tape
acrylic paints
stencil brush
paintbrush
black marker
two 38" (¾") dowels
screw hooks for wall mounting

Turn under 1" of canvas on side edges and hem. On top and bottom edges, turn under 1¾" of fabric and stitch 1½" from fold to form casings.

Make acetate stencils from all patterns except Santa. (*Note:* Cut separate stencils for the house and the smoke). Following photograph, position moon and star corner designs. To hold pieces of star in place, use small rolls of masking tape under the acetate

cutouts. Apply paint in an up-and-down motion of the stencil brush. Each time stencil is moved, wipe acetate clean with a damp rag.

At one end of the hanging, position a house stencil centered horizontally and so that the bottom of the house is in line with the top of the corner designs. Stencil house. Color should be heaviest along edge of stencil and gradually lighter toward center. Then stencil the smoke. On either side of this center house, stencil 2 trees with a house between. Repeat for other end of hanging.

Transfer pattern for Santa to center of hanging. (He is not stenciled.) Using bag stencils, paint outside edges of bags only. Outline Santa and bags with the felt-tip marker and paint solid colors according to photograph. For shaded areas, use marker lightly. Stencil reindeer around Santa as shown in photograph.

Insert dowels in top and bottom casings, and use screw hooks to hang.

REINDEER ON DOWELS:
pattern on page 127
5 ft. of 1″ x 8″ pine shelving
band or jigsaw
drill with ¼″ bit
wood glue
sandpaper
wood stain (optional)
ribbon (optional)
bells (optional)
36″ of ¼″ doweling

Transfer reindeer pattern to wood and cut out. Drill a hole in underside of each reindeer and sand entire piece. Cut a 30″ x 6″ piece of pine as a base. Drill three holes in base (10″ apart) and sand. Cut 3 lengths of dowels: 9″, 12″, and 15″. Apply glue to other end of dowel and insert in bottom of reindeer. Apply glue to other end of dowel and insert into base. If desired, stain reindeer, dowels, and base. To decorate, tie ribbon and bells around reindeer neck.

WOODEN HOUSE AND TREE CANDLE HOLDER:

pattern on page 127
18" (1" x 6") pine shelving for base
7½" x 18½" (⅛"-thick) plywood
band saw
drill with ¼" bit
wood glue
sandpaper
red, green, and white acrylic paint
votive candles
17½" (¼"-thick) doweling

Transfer house, tree, and chimney with smoke patterns to plywood and cut out. Drill ¼" holes randomly in tree shapes. Cut out windows and arch from house shape. For window sills and door brace, cut 3 (1¼" x ¼") pieces from plywood. Cut doweling into 2 (5¼") lengths for trees, and 2 (3½") lengths for house. Sand all pieces.

Paint window sills and door brace white, and chimney with smoke according to pattern. Glue chimney with smoke shape to right back side of house, window sills flush with bottom edge of windows, and door brace below door arch. Glue dowels to center back of each tree and to the outer back edges of the house, allowing ¼" of dowel to extend below figures. Let dry. Drill holes for dowels ½" in from front edge of base. Sand base and paint white. Paint trees and house according to pattern. Insert dowels into holes in base. Place candles behind shapes.

DECORATE WITH NATURE'S LITTLE EXTRAS

Nature provides a fascinating variety of stimulating materials for making gifts and decorations, and they are yours for the picking. Gather her bounty and start right away to make the natural creations presented here.

A sweet-gum bear (below) extends an open-pawed holiday greeting, and on the following pages are a pinecone valance—an incredibly simple, yet festive window trim; a charming little nutshell mouse with pointed ears and a quirky tail; a handsome box made from plywood and covered in orderly rows of pinecone scales; and finally, a wreath of vines and lichens inhabited by disarming peach pit ducks.

SWEET-GUM BEAR:
3 (3" x 4" x 8") blocks Oasis (florist's foam)
¼" dowels
Velverette glue
sweet-gum balls
felt (scrap)
25" (2½"-wide) red ribbon
florist's wire

(instructions continued)

Place 1 block on end for bear body. Cut another block in half for head (should be a square), and, with a paring knife, round off corners. To attach head to body, insert dowels and glue.

For arms and legs, cut third block into 2" x 3" x 4" quarters. Shorten arms 1". Shape, cut right-angled notches, and attach to corners of block as above.

From the remaining half-block, cut 2 ears (¾" x 3" x 4") and a nose (2" x 3" x 3"). Cut 3 pieces to round sides and back of head (1" x 1" x 3"). Shape all parts with knife to give bear desired roundness, and attach with dowels and glue as above.

To round sides of body, cut pieces 1½" x 3" x 4". The stomach is 2" x 3½" x 4". Round pieces and attach as for head and limbs. Allow glue to dry 24 hours.

Working from the bottom up, cover small areas of the bear with glue and push sweet-gum balls into the Oasis. Allow to dry another 24 hours.

Cut felt to fit bottom of bear and glue. Tie red ribbon in a bow and attach to neck with florist's wire.

PINECONE VALANCE:
15 large pinecones
red satin ribbon
3" wide felt ribbon (for bows and
  streamers)
thumbtacks
greenery (for top of window)

Cut different lengths of satin ribbon and staple or tie them to the top of the pinecones. Thumbtack ribbon ends above window. Place greenery on top of window to decorate and cover ribbon ends. Tie large felt ribbon bows and streamers and tack to window frame.

WALNUT MOUSE:
walnut shell half
cardboard
craft glue
2 small seashells or nut shells
3 small black beads
florist's wire
2" gold braid
clear varnish spray (mat finish)
gold glitter

To make mouse body, place flat side of walnut shell on cardboard and trace. Cut shape from cardboard and glue to shell.

At pointed end of mouse body, glue on shell ears, bead eyes, and nose. Cut 2" of florist's wire. Thread through gold braid to stiffen it. Twist braid to curl tail and glue to rounded end of body. Spray-paint mouse with clear varnish and sprinkle with glitter. Spray with varnish again.

13

PEACHY DUCK WREATH:
bread dough (recipe follows)
red and white acrylic paint
peach pits
flat-ended toothpicks
craft glue
6" vine wreath
lichens

BREAD DOUGH (makes several duck heads):
3 slices white bread
3 tablespoons craft glue
1 teaspoon glycerine
1 tablespoon green acrylic paint
3 drops lemon juice

Let bread sit out 2 hours before removing crust. Break into small pieces and, using hands, mix with other ingredients. (If you're not going to make duck heads right away, refrigerate dough in plastic bag until ready to use.)

To make heads, roll small amounts of dough into ¼" balls, break off flat ends of toothpicks and insert, rounded end out, in heads for bills. Allow about 24 hours to let dough dry. Dot red paint on heads for eyes and lightly brush white paint on top of peach pits for feathered effect. Glue heads to pits.

Glue lichens to vine wreath, then glue ducks on lichens.

PINECONE BOX:
scraps of plywood
nails
hammer
pinecone scales
glue gun

Nail plywood scraps together to form a box. Separate scales from pinecone. Trim ragged edge to make a flat edge. Apply glue to back of pinecone scale and press onto top edge of box, allowing rounded end of scale to extend about ⅛" above top. Continue this process around entire box.

Begin second row the same way, allowing top of second row to overlap and cover bottom edges of top row. Continue until entire box is covered. Let glue dry thoroughly.

15

COUNTRY PINES QUILT

Just as you once transformed notebook paper into a row of paperdolls holding hands, you can snip this country pines pattern from layered fabric and unfold a Christmas quilt appliqué.

This 27"-square quilt is a handsome accent spread on the table, hung on the wall, or displayed anywhere you want the warmth of fabric with a holiday flavor.

YOU WILL NEED:
pattern on page 128
18½" square of red cotton fabric
1 yd. green cotton fabric
⅜ yd. plaid cotton fabric
28" square of quilt batting
28" square of cotton backing fabric
heavy-weight red thread

Prewash and iron fabric. All measurements include a ¼" seam allowance.

Cut a 16" square from green fabric and fold as in Figures 1, 2, and 3. Press folded square to make sharp creases. Position pattern on folded green fabric as in Figure 4 and transfer. Baste inside pattern lines and along all folds. With very sharp scissors, cut on pattern lines through all layers. Remove basting and unfold.

Fold and press red square as above. Unfold red fabric and pin trees on it, matching center points and creases. Baste ½" inside edges. Remove pins and press out creases. Turn edges under ¼" and slip-stitch to background. Remove basting.

For borders, cut four 2" x 20½" plaid strips and four 3½" x 27" green strips. With right sides facing, stitch each green strip to a plaid one. With right sides facing, sew plaid strips to red background fabric at top and bottom. Stitch remaining border pieces to sides of background fabric, but do not sew into the top or bottom borders. Press seams toward inside. To miter corners, fold side borders under at corners, at a 45° angle. Press and slip-stitch over top and bottom border pieces. Trim excess fabric to ¼" underneath.

Sandwich square, batting, and backing. Allow batting and backing to extend 1" all around. To secure layers, baste together in a grid pattern and around edges. With red thread on red background, quilt around tree appliqués, very close to edges. Continue to outline-quilt tree appliqués with rows ½" apart to cover background. Inside appliqué, quilt trunks and branches.

Quilt green border in ½" rows that follow the angle of the mitered corners. Leave an open triangle in center of each green section of border. Do not quilt plaid border.

Trim excess batting and backing. From green fabric, cut four 1¾" x 27" binding strips. With right sides facing, stitch to front of quilted piece. Fold over to back. Turn under edges and slip-stitch to backing.

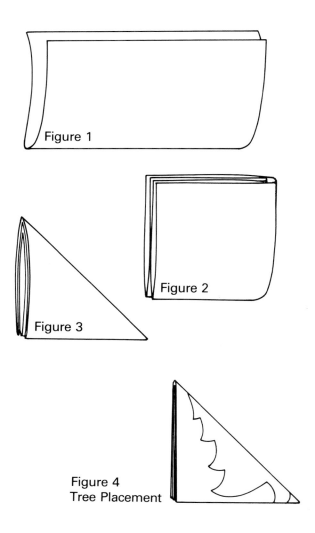

Figure 1

Figure 2

Figure 3

Figure 4
Tree Placement

LAST-MINUTE DECORATING: USE WHAT YOU HAVE

Here and on the following pages are last-minute decorations using accessories that you may have on hand. Look around your home for inspiration. As you will see, the accessories can be utilitarian or decorative. Gather collectibles with common materials or motifs. And consider household objects that you use every day. Choose a location for your arrangement where it will be easily seen and will receive flattering light. Move individual pieces around until you are pleased with the composition. To introduce the colors of the season, add some ribbons,

greenery, flowers, or whatever strikes your fancy, to create a one-of-a-kind display.

Below, a collection of antique, green glass bottles and jars and red carnations, provides subtle Christmas color. The composition forms a pyramid—the tallest bottles and longest-stemmed flowers are in the center, and the sizes graduate downward to the sides. Grouped on a beveled glass mirror to unify the arrangement, the water-filled containers catch and reflect the light. Dramatize this aspect for evening by adding votive candles in glass holders.

At right, a candle in a hurricane shade becomes an unusual decoration when ringed with pears and pine. A tin bucket holding pine cuttings, and a carved balsa-wood reindeer scoop filled with chestnuts, complete the appealingly understated grouping.

Below right, an old black kettle, blue-and-white kettle cloth, handcrafted copper utensils, dried okra, a shy wooden cow—this assortment imparts country charm to the red and green floral arrangement. Look around the house for things with a common bond such as style, material, motif, or color.

19

Above, brass, brass everywhere reflects the colors and lights of the season—in the candlesticks, doorknobs, andirons, even the hinges of the table. Above right, transform a mantel into an enchanted forest with a collection of brass figures surrounded by greenery. Tie ribbon bows around the neck of each animal.

At right, the magic of metallics is at its best in the warmth of copper and brass, as illustrated in this clustering of everyday kitchen accessories—a kettle, a pepper mill, a colander, a funnel, a big bucket, and a covered bowl. Bows of metallic ribbon trim the top of a tree that provides a backdrop for the arrangement. Lighted candles in brass holders set the metal surfaces a-shimmering.

A TRIO OF WOODEN ELVES

Need some extra assistance around the holidays? Try this wooden trio of Santa's helpers. Grouped together, they provide a buffet, mantel, or window decoration. Separately (and made with exterior-grade plywood), they can line the walkway leading to your front door, welcoming guests with every step.

YOU WILL NEED:
patterns on pages 130-131
3' of 1" x 12" pine shelving (For outside use, substitute masonite or exterior-grade plywood.)
sandpaper
wood sealer
gloss enamel paints (white, red, black, yellow, skin tone)
paintbrushes
3 (#8) 1¾" flathead wood screws
band saw or jigsaw

Transfer patterns to wood and cut out. Sand all surfaces. Paint with sealer. Let dry. Transfer painting details and paint as directed.

Cut a 5" circle from shelving for each base. Sand, paint with sealer, and when dry, paint green. Mount base to figure by screwing through base bottom and into the figure.

SANTA'S TINY HELPERS

Little hands are just the right size for roll-ing the felt pieces that construct these tiny people. Let your own small helpers make these Santa's helpers. You can do the cut-ting, and let them do the gluing. Chances are, you've got the materials needed tucked away in your scrap box.

Wrap a piece of ribbon around a curtain ring and glue on an elf for a tree ornament, or decorate a package with an elf couple.

Or glue a safety pin to the back to make an ornament to wear.

YOU WILL NEED (for 1 ornament):
2" x 3½" piece of red or green felt
glue gun or craft glue
10mm wooden bead head
pipe cleaner
yellow or brown yarn for hair
21" thin gold braid
scraps of ribbon
3" plastic curtain ring

Cut a 1½"-diameter felt circle; cut in half. Roll 1 half circle into a cone shape. Slightly overlap and glue straight edges together. For body, glue pointed end of cone to bead head. Cut one ½" x 1½" felt piece; roll into a tube for sleeves and glue along long edge. Glue center of tube to back of body. Cut one ½" x 2" felt piece; roll into a tube for pants and glue along long edge. Fold in half and glue inside body cone.

Cut four 1½" lengths from pipe cleaner and fold in half. Glue ends inside sleeves and pants legs. Folded ends will form hands and feet. Glue loops of yarn to bead head for hair. For a hat, roll other half of felt cir-cle into cone. Slightly overlap and glue straight edges together. Glue open end to bead head.

Use elves as ornaments or package deco-rations. Or, for an elf in a wreath, wrap gold braid around a curtain ring and glue ends to secure. Glue elf to bottom of ring and tie bow at top.

25

TRIM WITH SHIMMERING RIBBONS

Waves of golden ribbon, accenting the flame moiré wreath, stockings, and tree skirt, reflect the glow of brass candlesticks and tree ornaments here. At night, with candles burning, tree lights on, and fireplace ablaze, this room will shimmer.

Sophisticated, yes, but these decorations are designed to be simple, too. Ironed ribbon bows become appliqués for the stockings and tree skirt, and a wreath form blooms with looped ribbon and a cascade of golden bows.

WREATH:
10" Styrofoam (craft foam) wreath form
10 yds. (½"-wide) gold metallic ribbon
30 yds. (1½"-wide) red metallic ribbon
350 (1½"-long) U-shaped florist's pins
tape
florist's wire

Wrap gold ribbon around wreath to cover form. Pin end of red ribbon to inner circle of form, make a 1½" loop, and secure ribbon with pin next to first pin as shown in Figure. Continue making loops until a row circles inside of form. Remove first pin and pin the bases of the last and first loop together. Repeat this procedure to form a row next to the first row and continue to cover entire wreath (about 7 rows).

With gold ribbon, make several bows and secure to bottom of wreath with florist's pin. To form hanger, wrap florist's wire around top of form so that loops hide it, and twist into circle on back.

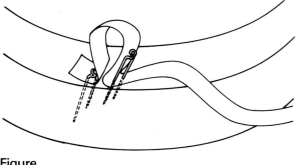

Figure

STOCKINGS (for 3 stockings):
pattern on page 144
1½ yds. red moiré fabric
thread to match
3 yds. piping cord
3 yds. (½"-wide) metallic ribbon

Transfer and cut out 3 stocking patterns. Reverse and cut out 3 more. From remaining fabric, cut ½" bias strips and sew together for three 1-yd. lengths (1 yd. per stocking). Cut piping cord into 1-yd. lengths, fold bias strips around cord, and sew. With right sides of front and back stocking pieces facing, pin piping between layers with raw edges of piping aligned with raw edges of stocking pieces. (At corners, clip raw edges of piping, being careful not to clip through seam.) Stitch layers together and turn. Fold top of stocking under 1" and hem.

To make loop for hanging, cut a 1" x 4" strip of fabric. Fold lengthwise, right sides facing, and stitch along long edge with ¼" seam allowance. Turn, fold in half, and tack ends to inside back of stocking. Make a bow from metallic ribbon, and press to shape following photograph. Tack to stocking.

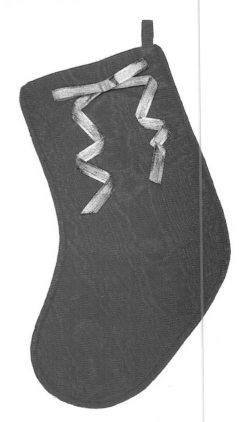

TREE SKIRT:

4⅛ yds. (45"-wide) red moiré fabric
½ yd. matching fabric for bias strip (optional)
7 yds. piping cord (optional)
thread to match
6½ yds. (½"-wide) metallic ribbon

Cut fabric into two 2-yd. pieces and, with a ¼" seam allowance, baste them together lengthwise. Fold the fabric in half twice to form quarters.

Working from corner with no raw edges, draw a quarter-circle arc with a 36" radius. (See Figure 1.) Pin layers together, and cut along curve with sharp scissors.

From same corner, mark a quarter-circle arc with a 1½" radius (Figure 2), and cut to form opening for tree. Open skirt, remove basting from 1 side of skirt (for opening),

and stitch along line of basting on other side. Press seam open.

Hem skirt or pipe, as desired. Use purchased piping or make it yourself. To make a 7-yd. bias strip, cut 1½"-wide strips from extra ½ yd. of fabric and sew ends together. Wrap fabric around piping cord and pin or baste to right side of edge of skirt, with raw edges aligned and cord toward center of skirt. Sew seam close to cord and trim excess fabric. Hem raw edges of skirt.

For skirt's ties, cut two 3" x 18" pieces of fabric and fold lengthwise, right sides facing. With a ¼" seam allowance, sew one short end and the long side of each tie, and turn. Turn edges of remaining end to inside and slip-stitch closed. Attach a tie to each edge of skirt opening.

Make bows from metallic ribbon and press to shape. Tack to skirt.

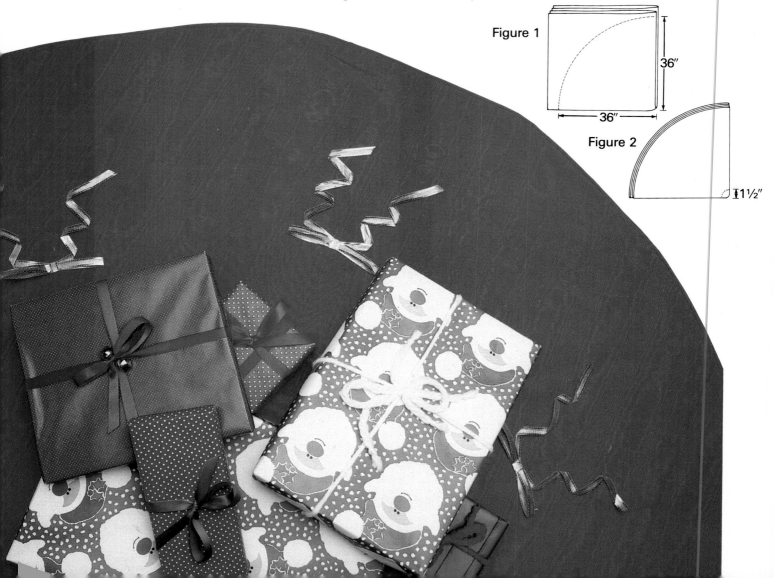

Figure 1

36"

36"

Figure 2

1½"

APPLE CANDLESTICKS

If you don't have all the candlesticks you need to celebrate the holidays with candlelight, or if you want to decorate the candlesticks you do have with festive color, apples are the answer.

To make candlesticks from apples, choose fruit that is fresh and unbruised. Be sure that each apple is balanced when set on its bottom, and that the core appears to be vertically straight. Polish apples with a soft cloth until they shine. With a sharp knife or apple corer, core the apple. Insert a candle and tie a bow around the candle at the top of the apple.

To top an existing candlestick, push the candle all the way through the apple and into the socket in the candlestick. Apple candlesticks should last a week or more.

QUIET ELEGANCE FOR THE HOLIDAYS

If bold reds and greens, bright lights, and tinsel are not your style, consider this delicate option. Lace, baby's breath, and pastel taffeta suggest the quiet elegance of days gone by. Imagine your relief at returning to this haven after a hectic day of shopping.

Miniature wreaths and lacy ribbon roses sit amid baby's breath on the evergreen wreath and tree. White net makes glass ornaments look as though they hold frosty morning air, and opulent diamond-shaped ornaments are no more than lace and trinkets over paper forms. To complete the effect, a gracefully scalloped skirt of rose and ecru moiré encircles the tree. Instructions for these decorations follow.

MOIRÉ AND LACE TREE SKIRT:
pattern on page 135
1¼ yds. (45"-wide) ecru moiré taffeta
½ yd. (45"-wide) rose taffeta
ecru thread
2½ yds. (1¼"-wide) gathered ecru lace
5 yds. (2½"-wide) gathered ecru lace
6 yds. (1¾"-wide) lace-edged ecru moiré ribbon
6 yds. (⅞"-wide) rose floral ribbon

Cut a 45"-diameter circle from ecru fabric and fold in half 3 times to divide circle in eighths. To scallop the edge, place scallop pattern on folded fabric as pattern indicates, and cut. Unfold fabric and cut a 3½"-diameter circle in center. From a point at which two scallops meet, cut fabric in a straight line to the center circle.

Transfer patterns for insets and appliqués to rose fabric, and cut out.

Zigzag-stitch edges of skirt. Repeat for insets. Baste rose appliqués to skirt and machine-satin-stitch around outlines.

Topstitch 1¼"-wide lace to scalloped edges of insets. Position insets around skirt with the skirt overlapping them ¼", and topstitch. Topstitch 2½"-wide lace to scalloped edge of ecru skirt. Hem the remaining raw

edges. With lace-edged ecru ribbon and floral ribbon together, make 7 bows. Tack to
skirt where scallop appliqués meet.

NET-FILLED GLASS BALL ORNAMENTS:

Remove hanger top from clear glass balls
and stuff with net. Replace top and glue ribbon or lace around side of top to cover.
Glue ribbon and tiny silk flowers on top.

To recycle old colored balls, fill with chlo-
rine bleach, allow to sit for a few minutes,
and then rinse out the paint lining. Repeat if
necessary until ball is clear.

DIAMOND LACE ORNAMENT (for 1):
pattern on page 148
poster paper
craft glue
rubber cement
4 (3" x 8") scraps of fabric
2 yds. lace and ribbon trim
trinkets for decoration
heavy gold twine or cord
gold tassel

Transfer pattern to poster paper and cut
out. Lightly score folding lines and fold into
diamond shape with flaps to the outside.
Apply glue to flaps, slip to inside, and hold
ornament together until dry.

Apply rubber cement to top, middle, and
bottom parts of 1 section of ornament, and
smooth a piece of fabric over the section so
that fabric extends beyond all edges. When
dry, trim fabric along edges of section. Repeat for remaining 3 sections.

Glue trim over fabric edges with craft glue
and decorate with trim and trinkets as desired. For a hanger, thread 8" of gold cord
through top and tie. Attach tassel to bottom
of ornament.

EVERGREEN WREATH
WITH LACY ORNAMENTS

To make the evergreen wreath, take 8" to
12" cuttings from the tree or bush, being
careful not to damage the shape of the plant.
On a raffia, craft foam, or wire wreath form,
hold branches (as many as necessary to

cover the wreath at that point) in place. Secure stem ends to the wreath form by wrapping with florist's wire. Next, lay branches in
same direction, with leafy ends covering
stems and wire of first. Wire these branches
in place as before. Continue process to cover
entire wreath.

LACY WREATH ORNAMENT:
wooden ring (3" diameter)
saw
3" x 12" strip of fabric
12" (1"-wide) lace
brass screw eye
ribbon trim (optional)

Cut through wooden ring at one point.
With right sides facing, fold fabric in half
lengthwise. Pin lace between layers with 1
edge aligned with raw edges of fabric. Stitch
all layers with 1/8" seam, leaving ends open.
Turn right side out, and forcing wooden ring
open at cut, slide casing onto ring.

For a hanger, screw brass eye where open
ends of fabric casing meet. If desired, tie a
ribbon bow and tack to bottom of ornament.

RIBBON ROSES:

Directions are for 5/8"-wide ribbon. Measurements may vary for different widths of
ribbon.

Cut 6" to 8" of ribbon, and fold in half
lengthwise. Fold 1 1/2" of ribbon downward to
form a 90° angle (see Figure). Hold short end
with right hand and, with left hand, wrap
longer end tightly around fold. Take several
stitches through flower base to secure.

Continue wrapping ribbon, twisting as you
go, and let ribbon get looser so that flower
appears to open. When flower is the desired
fullness, wrap thread very tightly around
base and stitch to secure. Trim remaining
thread and ribbon.

Figure.

ACCENTS OF LACE AND EMBROIDERY

The feminine touches seen here comple- ment a lacy seasonal decor, then confer ele- gance year round. A mauve fan embroidered on moiré taffeta makes an accent piece that echoes the romance of Victorian times. Let it adorn a corner of your home or wrap it up for a sentimental friend.

For Christmas soirées or brunches, add re- finement to your table with napkins ringed by lace. To carry the elegant theme one step further, cup the servings with shaped lace. Just cut inexpensive lace to the desired size, soak it in liquid starch, and place it in what- ever container will give the appropriate con- tour. Allow the lace to dry thoroughly, then carefully remove it. For candies or petit fours, try a cupcake pan. Ice cream dishes work well for larger servings.

And old-fashioned charm will set your gifts apart when they're tied with lace and crowned by a nosegay of lace and silk flow- ers. For a one-of-kind corsage, replace the nosegay's silk flowers with real rosebuds. It's easy to keep rosebuds fresh through even the longest holiday event. Just insert florist's wire through freshly cut stems, place wet pieces of cotton balls over each stem end, and wrap florist's tape around the cotton and stems.

Instructions are on the next page.

EMBROIDERED LACE FAN:

patterns and color key on page 135
⅓ yd. mauve moiré taffeta
embroidery floss (see color key)
8" (⅝"-wide) mauve satin ribbon
½ yd. (⅛"-wide) light green satin ribbon

Transfer fan pattern to the mauve taffeta. Refer to the color key for floss colors and stitches.

Work all parts of design with 4 strands of floss, except the following: For French knots on scallops and scroll work, use 6 strands of floss. To embroider bullion knot roses, use 4 strands of wine floss for center 3 knots. Use 6 strands of mauve floss for a second set of 3 knots overlapping the first set. Then for the outermost set of 3 knots, use 6 strands of pale mauve floss, overlapping the second group of knots.

To embroider the scalloped top border, backstitch outlines, then satin-stitch over backstitching. Block finished embroidery.

Make a double bow with green ribbon, curling ribbon ends by pulling quickly along sharp edge of scissors. Glue to base of fan as shown in photograph. To make a mauve ribbon rose, see instructions on page 32. Glue rose to center of bow.

Have embroidery framed or frame it yourself. If desired, wrap a purchased frame or a mat with coordinating fabric and lace.

LACE NOSEGAY:

16" (2½"-wide) lace
thread to match
purchased silk flowers with wire stems
⅛" to ¾"-wide scraps of ribbon and lace
   (colors desired)

Baste along 1 long edge of 2½" lace, gather tightly, and stitch basted corners together to form a circle. Cut stems of flowers to 6", and insert through center opening of lace. Twist stems together and form a circle for hanging. Make bows from ribbon and lace scraps and stitch to lace opening around flowers.

LACE NAPKIN RINGS (for 4 napkin rings):

28" (2½"-wide) lace
liquid starch
fabric glue
4 silk rosebuds with wire stems
28" (½"-wide) ribbon (color desired)

Cut lace into four 7" lengths. Starch, following manufacturer's instructions to obtain maximum stiffness. When dry, loop into circle with a 1" overlap and glue ends together.

Cut four 7" lengths of ribbon and tie in bows around rosebud's stem at base of bud. Cut stem so that 2" remain below bow, slip stem through lace opposite glued side, and twist to secure.

WINDOW SNOWFLAKES

Maybe you have an heirloom collection of doilies and other small needlework pieces that have been passed down through your family; or perhaps you've purchased some pretty handmade pieces from flea markets or antique stores; or possibly you've participated in the needle-arts revival—crochet, tatting, net darning—and have sampler circles or squares of your own making. Showcase these decorative needlework pieces by framing them, sandwiched between glass, and hanging them in a window like giant suspended snowflakes. Use frames of the same material and border width.

FRAGRANT TABLETOP TREES

When you enter the room where this tree stands, the first thing you may notice is a faint but intriguing aroma, the come-hither scents of dried flowers, herbs, and various other plant materials. The tree shown here was made with artemisia and trimmed with pepper berries, strawflowers, roses, statice, hydrangea, globe amaranth, love-in-a-mist, and money plant.

This tree and the ones on the following pages were designed by members of the Herb Society of Worthington, Ohio. The setting is the Worthington Inn, a restored 1831 stagecoach stopover. Furnished with Ohio antiques, it is a rich backdrop for these delicate decorations.

The community of Worthington has several very active clubs, including the Herb Society, the Garden Club, and the Historical Society, all of whom work together to bring the look of Christmas to their town. In addition to decorating the inn for the holidays, the citizens of Worthington also trim the downtown streets elaborately, and host a number of special events, including a colonial Christmas party for children, at another historic site, the Orange-Johnson House, built in 1816.

Members of the Herb Society of Worthington offer these tips for creating a tree with dried materials. Gather herbs, flowers, and other plants at the height of the growing season. To dry, hang them upside down in a cool, dry place. Or lay them in a box, carefully cover with silica gel, and cover with a lid. Drying times vary. When the plant cutting is brittle, it should be ready to use.

For the tree base, you'll need a craft foam cone. To cover this form, use a plant with thick, pretty foliage and stems strong enough to push into the foam. Insert the stems into the foam and glue to secure. (If you have one, a glue gun is ideal for this application.) Add accent materials with contrasting color and textures. Be sure to include some materials that add fragrance.

Above, a tabletop tree is at just the right height to enjoy up close. Covered with a type of artemisia known as Sweet Annie, this herb tree is trimmed with tansy, blue salvia, Queen Anne's lace, cockscomb, bells of Ireland, ammobium, and hydrangea.

Right, backed by a punched-tin pie safe in a kitchen, this little tree was made with Silver King artemisia—a variety that has soft green, silver-dusted leaves when dried. Rose hips provide striking contrast to the foliage.

SILHOUETTE THE SEASON

Here's a winter scene that will add another character to your children's Christmas—Skating Bunny. Framed with icicles, this window silhouette will create another dimension for your decorating, too. Make one to go in each child's window for a pleasing view—whether seen from the inside or out.

A bit of greenery and candles at the top of the design will cover uneven edges.

Another aspect of this pattern is its adaptability. In addition to making a window hanging, the pattern may be used to stencil a rug, quilt a throw pillow, or to make your own wrapping paper design.

YOU WILL NEED:
pattern on page 134
⅛"-wide foam-core board
craft or mat knife with extra blades

Measure your window and enlarge pattern accordingly, adding to borders as necessary for pattern to fit proportionately. Transfer pattern to foam core and cut out. Do not attempt to cut through board with one motion. Score several times along the same line for a neat cut. Should foam core begin to tear rather than cut, the blade is too dull and should be changed.

WEAVE SOME CHRISTMAS CHARM

This Christmas, involve your children in a project that requires simple materials and minimum supervision. Younger children may require help in cutting out patterns and weaving lines, but the assembly process is quite easy. Tie the ornaments to Christmas packages for an "I made it myself" touch.

TIPS ON FELT AND RIBBON WEAVING: Before beginning to weave, pin the felt piece to Styrofoam or cork to secure. To weave, insert ribbon over and under, over and under, etc., through openings cut in felt. On the next row, alternate by weaving under and over, under and over, etc. Continue alternating with each row. Glue ribbon ends to the front edge of felt piece and trim. (If desired, the back piece may also be woven if you cut weaving lines in it and double the amount of ribbon.)

TREE ORNAMENT:
pattern on page 129
6" x 6½" piece green felt
6" x 6½" piece yellow felt
1 yd. (¼"-wide) yellow satin ribbon
1 yd. (¼"-wide) green satin ribbon
40" (⅛"-wide) red satin ribbon
craft glue
fiberfill

Pin felt pieces together. Transfer pattern to felt and cut out both pieces at once. Remove pattern and separate felt. Cut weaving lines on green felt (front) according to pattern.

Begin weaving at top of tree with yellow ribbon. Alternate rows with green ribbon. Weave 4 rows in top and middle sections, and 5 rows in bottom section. To make a loop for hanging, cut a 4" length of green ribbon. Glue both ends of ribbon to back of tree top, with loop extending above tree top. Cut eight 5" lengths of red ribbon, tie bows, and set aside. Cut a 6" length of yellow ribbon, tie a bow, and set aside.

To assemble, apply glue to top back of tree (¼" from edge) down edges to first indentation. Match to same area on yellow felt back and allow glue to dry. Stuff top section with fiberfill and seal with curved horizontal line of glue, according to pattern. Repeat for middle and bottom sections. Finish gluing bottom of tree, leaving trunk section open. Stuff and seal trunk. Glue the red ribbons to the 6 side points of the tree and in 2 places in the middle of tree. Glue the yellow ribbon to the top of the tree.

ANGEL ORNAMENT:
pattern on page 129
8" square lavender felt
8" square hot pink felt
1⅔ yds. (¼"-wide) light pink satin ribbon
craft glue
1 yd. (⅜"-wide) hot pink satin ribbon
1½ yds. (⅛"-wide) light pink satin ribbon
30" (⅛"-wide) white satin ribbon
fiberfill

Pin felt squares together. Transfer pattern to felt and cut out both pieces of felt at once. Remove pattern and separate felt pieces. Cut weaving lines on lavender felt piece (front) according to pattern.

Start at the wing with ¼"-wide pink ribbon, and weave 6 rows. Glue and trim ribbon ends as you work. Repeat for opposite wing. To weave dress, begin at the neck with a row of hot pink ribbon. Weave next row with light pink ribbon. Alternate colors with each row for a total of 12 rows. To make the eyes, cut two 5" pieces of ⅛" pink

ribbon. Tie 2 bows, trim the edges so bows are very small and glue on angel face. To make a loop for hanging, cut a 4" length of ⅛"-wide pink ribbon. Glue both ends to center back of head, with loop extending above head.

Cut 1 yard of ⅛" pink ribbon into three 12" lengths. Hold ends even, tie a knot in one end and braid the 3 lengths of ribbon. Tie another knot at the end to hold braid. Find the center of braid and glue it to the top center of the angel head. Glue braid to side of angel head, but leave lower section of braids loose. Cut five 5" lengths of white ribbon and tie 5 bows. Glue bows to ends of braids, and to wing tips and neck.

To assemble, apply glue around outside of head (¼" from edge) on back side, match to same area on pink felt back, and allow glue to dry. Stuff head with fiberfill and seal neck with a horizontal line of glue, as indicated on pattern. To make a halo, cut a 5" length of white ribbon. Glue the ends together, making a circle, and attach to sides toward the top of head. Allow ribbon to extend loosely outward. Glue top and scalloped edges of wing front and back piece. Stuff wing and seal with diagonal line of glue, according to pattern. Repeat for other wing. Glue sides of dress and bottom of angel, leaving a 2" opening. Stuff and seal opening.

BELL ORNAMENT:
pattern on page 129
6½" x 5½" piece of magenta felt
6½" x 5½" piece of pink felt
20" (¼"-wide) lavender satin ribbon
1⅓ yds. (¼"-wide) green satin ribbon
24" (¼"-wide) white satin ribbon
craft glue
fiberfill

Pin felt pieces together. Transfer pattern to felt and cut out both pieces of felt at once. Remove pattern and separate felt. Cut weaving lines on magenta felt (front) according to pattern.

Start at top of bell with lavender ribbon, and weave 2 rows of each color ribbon (with the exception of 1 row of white at the bottom). Allow ribbon to curve slightly as you work down the bell. Glue and trim ribbon ends as you work. To make a loop for hanging, cut a 4" length of green ribbon. Glue both ends of ribbon to top back of bell, with loop extending above top of bell.

To assemble, glue woven front (apply glue ¼" from edge) to pink felt back along edges. Leave a 2" opening at bottom for stuffing. Allow glue to dry completely. Stuff bell and seal the opening.

STOCKING ORNAMENT:
pattern on page 128
5" x 8½" piece of green felt
5" x 8½" piece of turquoise felt
½ yd. (¼"-wide) white satin ribbon
1⅓ yd. (¼"-wide) hot pink satin ribbon
½ yd. (⅛"-wide) white satin ribbon
craft glue
fiberfill

Pin felt squares together. Transfer pattern to felt and cut out both pieces at once. Remove pattern and separate felt. Cut weaving lines on green felt (front) according to the pattern.

Start at the top and weave 4 rows of white ribbon. Glue and trim ribbon ends as you work. Next, weave 10 rows of hot pink ribbon. (The 6th row will extend diagonally from inside curve toward the heel but will not extend to the heel.) To make a loop for hanging, cut a 4" length of white ribbon. Glue both ends of ribbon to back of top left corner, with loop extending above stocking. Cut two 6" lengths of ⅛"-wide white ribbon and tie bows. Glue at heel and toe. Cut a 10" length of hot pink ribbon, tie a bow, and glue at top corner near hanging loop.

To assemble, apply glue to top and sides of first section of stocking (¼" from edge). Match to same area on turquoise felt back and allow glue to dry. Stuff and seal with a horizontal line of glue, as indicated on pattern. Continue gluing edges together, leaving a 2" opening for stuffing. Allow glue to dry. Stuff stocking and seal opening.

CELESTIAL CROSS-STITCH

Cross-stitch angels floating among snow-flakes can grace your tree this year. Here, pretty pastels and beadwork combine to form softly elegant ornaments.

Worked on 14-count Aida cloth, these ornaments are backed with felt and suspended from the branches with metallic thread. The angel in flight blows a gold-bead trumpet. A white wing, outlined in pearly beads, partly frames the praying angel nestled against a crescent moon.

To produce the illusion of a multitude of snowflake patterns, vary the colors of beading. The intricate patterns offer many possible combinations.

Consider beginning an annual tradition with these ornaments by cross-stitching the year on Aida cloth, and using that in place of the felt back. For added stiffness, bond the layers with fusible fabric.

YOU WILL NEED:
charts and color key on page 133
14-count Aida cloth
embroidery floss (see color key)
beads (see color key)
craft glue
fabric glue
felt
metallic thread

Work designs on Aida cloth according to charts.

Before cutting designs out, apply craft glue to the back, along outer edges of design, to prevent raveling. Let glue dry, then cut closely along glue line.

Spread fabric glue on back of cross-stitch design and place on felt. When glue is dry, cut away excess felt. For a hanger, sew metallic thread to top of ornament.

A GOODIE TREE

This tabletop tree, trimmed with tiny trea-sures, is a cone shaped from hardware cloth. Wire mesh provides a framework on which to fasten a variety of small decorative ob-jects. Ornaments, miniature toys, candy, and bows can be tied on with string. Attach ran-domly, leaving spaces that reveal the un-usual foundation, or cover the entire tree. To let friends and neighbors (especially little ones) know that you appreciate their visits, keep a pair of scissors handy and invite them to snip a take-home treat from the tree. Just tie on more goodies when you need to re-plenish the supply.

To make the tree, cut a half-circle with a radius of 15″ from a 15″ x 30″ piece of hard-ware cloth (4 squares to the inch). Roll this half-circle into a cone and secure the edges with wire. Spray-paint desired color.

For a base, cut a plywood circle slightly larger than the bottom of the cone, and a smaller circle, from 1″ wood. Center the cir-cles and glue together. Place the base with the small circle down and center the cone on the base. Sketch around the bottom of the cone. Remove the cone and nail U-shaped tacks just inside this line. Twist 4″ lengths of wire around the tacks and bend the ends outward. Spray-paint the base. Cen-ter the cone on the base and twist wires around the mesh to secure. Tuck wires to the inside.

STARS GALORE!

One pattern produces all the celestial bodies shown on this tree. Just cut stars from poster paper (pattern is on page 132), tape string to the back, and you have the ornaments shown here and more. Their ease of construction makes them a project that children will enjoy, too.

Try cutting three stars, from large to small, and hanging them one below the other.

Hang small stars inside larger ones. Slot two stars and slip them together to create a three-dimensional ornament.

Various materials provide even more options. Wrap paper ornaments with aluminum foil and cast a stunning spell by placing them near lights. Try glitter, colored paper, fabric, lace . . . whatever will make these ornaments as personal as they are unique.

FESTIVE FELT

A new twist to the traditional Della Robbia-style wreath is this bright and easy array of fruits and leaves. Vivid colors set in a traditional wreath arrangement give this decoration the ability to fit any room.

Use it over a fireplace, on a door, in a window, or placed around a simple composition of candles to give them extra flair. And the fruit will be just as fresh when you take it down from the attic to use next year.

The individual fruits may be added to mantel arrangements of plain greenery, or to brighten a centerpiece. Or add a piece of string to the back and hang the single fruits on your tree for some original ornaments.

YOU WILL NEED:
patterns on page 125
⅔ yd. (72"-wide) kelly green felt
20" cardboard circle with 10" circle cut from the center
2¼ lb. package polyester stuffing
2 yds. kelly green yarn cut into 2" lengths
¼ yd. (60"-wide) felt in each color (red, yellow, orange, and plum)
9" x 16" piece deep purple felt
140 purple pom-poms (1" or 1½")
⅔ yd. (60"-wide) lime green felt
glue gun

Fold kelly green felt in half and cut out two 24" circles with 8" centers. Insert the 20"

cardboard circle between the 24" felt circles. With a ½" seam allowance, hand-stitch felt pieces together around center circle. Cut a small hole through back layer of felt and cardboard. Tie a length of yarn through hole for hanging wreath. Fill wreath with stuffing material, and using a ¼" seam allowance, stitch outer edges of felt circles together as you stuff.

Transfer patterns to fabric. Cut out 18 apples from red felt; 16 pears from yellow felt; 16 circles from orange felt; 16 circles from plum felt. Then cut 6 grape clusters from purple felt.

Stitch 2 apple pieces together around edges, leaving a small opening to stuff. Insert

a length of yarn for the stem. Follow this procedure for each piece of fruit (except grape clusters). Lightly stuff each and stitch openings closed. Glue approximately 22 pom-poms onto each grape piece to form grape clusters.

Cut out 30 lime green and 30 kelly green leaves. Place one lime and one kelly green leaf together. Stitch and stuff same as for fruit. Stitch lengthwise down the center to form a vein.

Glue fruit and leaves onto wreath covering entire front. Fruit and leaves may overlap.

HANDMADE WITH LOVE

A reassuring squeeze of the hand, a quick hug—these are sweet communications from loving hands. So, too, are handmade gifts. Created with care and tailored to individual needs and tastes, handcrafted presents are tangible evidence of your affection. Match gift ideas from the following pages with special people on your list, and begin a labor of love.

MAKE IT FUN TO WEAR

Do you remember a garment from your childhood that you loved to wear more than any other? Make these fun-to-wear play togs, with attention-getting embellishments, for your little ones. They may well become your child's favorite apparel.

With basic construction and quick smocking, this pretty pinafore is practical to make, even for everyday playwear. Make it from a length of gingham, and use the checks of the fabric as a smocking guide. Gather the top of the pinafore by joining the corners of each check with embroidery floss in a contrasting color. Complete the dress with shoulder and back ties.

The adorable teddy bear design, plush and tempting to touch, is done with a technique called punched needlework. Yarn is threaded through a hollow needle, which is plunged in and out of the fabric to make loops. When these loops are trimmed, a pile is formed that resembles real fur. Since the design is worked on a pocket, you can transfer it to a new garment when your child outgrows his clothes.

TEDDY BEAR POCKET:
pattern on page 132
5" x 10" woven fabric (kettle or weaver's cloth)
2-ply punch embroidery yarn (dark brown, light brown and pink)
1 punch embroidery needle (large-eyed)
interfacing (optional)
button eyes or plain buttons
6" or 8" embroidery hoop with lip

Transfer bear pattern to wrong side of fabric with bear's head 1" from short edge (Figure 1). (If using dark-colored fabric, transfer pattern to interfacing. Place interfacing with design side up on wrong side of fabric.) With fabric wrong side up, center design over small ring of hoop. Place large ring over fabric and small ring, and lock hoop tightly (Figure 2).

Adjust needle to a ¾" length. Thread with 6 strands of yarn. Punching from wrong side, begin with small areas (pink in paws and feet), keeping fingers close to stitching row. (If using interfacing, be sure to punch through both interfacing and fabric.) Work slowly in rows.

Complete a small area, turn work to front and clip across tops of loops. Trimming edges at an angle adds definition. Give special attention to detail areas (legs, arms, head, eyes). Trim around the eye area, leaving the opening slightly larger than the button eye to be used. Sew eyes in place.

Remove fabric from the hoop. Avoiding the design, iron fabric.

At top and bottom of pocket, turn ½" fabric under and stitch. Fold top to bottom, right sides facing. Stitch sides with ¼" seam, leaving top open. Turn pocket right side out and sew to garment along sides and bottom.

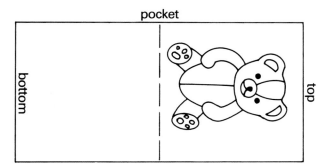

Figure 1—Position for Pattern

Figure 2—Positioning Fabric in Hoop

SMOCKED GINGHAM PINAFORE:
1 yd. (45"-wide) gingham
1 skein DMC embroidery floss
45" (½"-wide) lace
thread to match

Note: Pinafore fits sizes 4-5. Along straight line of fabric print, cut a 21" x 45" piece of fabric. Turn 1 long edge under ¼" and machine-stitch lace to inside edge. To smock, use the corners of the squares on material as guidelines. Start below first full squares under lace, and working left to right, stitch corners of every other square together, gathering pleats as you stitch. (See photo.) Smock entire width of fabric. Staggering stitches from previous row, repeat rows until smocking is 3½" deep.

The remaining long edge is the bottom of the pinafore. Hem to desired length. Fold selvage edges under ½" and stitch.

For back ties, cut 4 strips (1" x 10"). Fold in half lengthwise, right sides facing, and stitch ¼" seam, leaving one end open. Turn right side out. Turn under open ends ½" and stitch to sides of pinafore at top and bottom of smocking pattern.

To make shoulder straps, cut 4 straps (2¼" x 18"). Fold in half lengthwise, right sides facing, and stitch with ¼" seam, leaving one end open. Turn right side out; measure straps to fit and stitch open edge to inside top of pinafore, 2 for back 3½" from side edges of apron, and 2 for front, 9" from edges. Stitch again to secure.

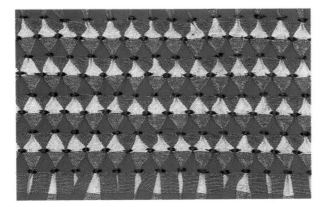

BABY'S FIRST CHRISTMAS

Christmas decorating in the baby's room is a delightful task requiring a little extra thought. Rather than using the normal red and green color schemes, choose Christmas motifs adapted to the pastel colors more often found in a baby's room.

A sprinkling of colors and twinkling of lights on this tree give the feeling of Christmas, while maintaining the delicacy of a nursery decor. After the holidays, place the tree in a corner of the room and use it as a nightlight.

The bell-shaped pincushion woven in pastel ribbon is another soft nursery accent. Just make it with Christmas colors, and you have a tree ornament. (Instructions, page 44.)

YOU WILL NEED:
22" x 28" poster board
19½" string
masking tape
2½ yds. (40"-wide) Dip 'N Drape fabric
gesso
drill with 7/32" bit
high-gloss, white spray paint
toothbrush
acrylic paint (green, yellow, red, blue)
eyedropper
50-count set of miniature Christmas lights

To make poster board base, tie string to a pencil, close to the point. Hold the other end of string in corner of poster board. Extend the string so that end with pencil is 19½" from secured point, and draw an arc (about ¼ circle). Cut along curved line. Measure 1½" from top point and cut a horizontal line to make a straight top.

Form into a cone and overlap edges leaving a ¼" hole in top of cone. Tape to secure. At the base, cut a small notch in edge for electric cord to pass through. From fabric, cut (5"-wide) strips in these lengths: 10", 13", 17", 22", 25", 28", 35", 36", 37". Fold strips lengthwise. Cut final strip of fabric ¾" x 5" and fold lengthwise in thirds.

Begin at bottom of cone with the longest strip. Prepare fabric for application by dipping a strip in water and quickly pulling it between your fingers to squeeze out excess water. (Fabric takes about 30 seconds to become pliable.) With creased edge down, press top ¼" of raw edge onto cone. Gather fabric as it is applied by pinching the raw edges together. Press the indentations in ruffle flush with cone, making a place to drill holes for lights.

As each row is completed, turn under ends of strips to hide raw edges. Continue adding strips, with each new row overlapping previous row enough to hide raw edges. Attach next to last strip ⅛" below top of cone. Final strip is not ruffled, but wrapped around the top, with raw edge folded under against cone to conceal edges of last ruffle. Let dry thoroughly.

Paint outside of cone with gesso. Let dry. Drill 49 random holes in tree at the indentations in ruffles. The ¼" hole in top of tree holds 50th light. Spray-paint tree white, being sure to cover under ruffles. Let dry.

To spatter-paint tree green, dip toothbrush in paint thinned with water. Pull thumb across bristles to throw tiny speckles of paint on tree. Use an eyedropper to squeeze yellow, red, and blue paint randomly for decorations. Let dry.

From inside of cone, insert lights through holes, beginning with the light farthest from the plug in the top hole, and work down. Tape lights in place inside cone.

TERRY THE SNOWMAN

Meet Terry the Snowman. If he catches you looking at him, he invariably smiles back warmly, and his black eyes twinkle. (No cold shoulders or icy stares here.) He's quite a charmer, and he knows it, as evidenced by his dashing (if minimal) attire. His plaid, wool muffler is knotted at the neck, with fringed ends falling jauntily to one side. And his dapper derby hat, made of black felt, is trimmed with a red satin band.

This personable snowman is easier to make than the real McCoy. Instead of rolling up icy balls of snow, roll up circles of terry cloth in graduated sizes, gathering and stuffing, stacking and stitching them to make the body. (No cold hands!) The eyes, nose, and of course, the buttons, are big, shiny buttons. The quirky mouth is stitched, and the arms are twiggy branches. These snowmen shape up quickly for Christmas gifts. And for party favors or ornaments, you can scale down the size of the terry-cloth circles.

Give Terry a visible post in your home—on the mantel, under the tree, in a window, as a centerpiece—and he'll warm hearts with his well-rounded personality.

YOU WILL NEED:
1 yd. white terry cloth
Scotchgard (protective spray for fabric)
heavy white thread
1 bag (16-ounce) fiberfill
5 (½"-diameter) black shank buttons
tacky glue
2 (5"-long) twigs (for arms)
3" x 22" scrap of wool flannel (for scarf)
7½" x 11½" black felt (for hat)
14" (⅝"-wide) ribbon (for hat)
small holly decoration

From terry cloth, cut 1 circle each of 16", 11½", and 10"-diameter. Treat with protective spray and let dry.

With heavy white thread, make a long running stitch ½" from edge of largest circle. Gather edge to form a ball. Stuff with fiberfill, pull tight to close, knot and clip thread.

Repeat for medium and small circles.

Sew the gathered ends of large and medium balls together. For the head, sew eyes, nose, and mouth to small ball.

Place twig arms on either side of medium ball where head is sure to cover them. Glue ends of twigs to ball. Let dry. Sew head to medium ball. Sew buttons on front of medium ball.

For scarf, stitch 1" from each end of flannel piece. Remove threads from stitching to end, to form a fringe. Fold lengthwise with right sides facing and sew edges together with ⅝" seam. Turn right side out and tie around neck.

To make the hat, cut out a 5"-diameter felt circle with a 2½" center opening for a brim. For sides of crown, cut a 2" x 11½" felt strip; overlap edges ¼" and glue. Let dry. For top of crown, cut out a felt circle 3¾" in diameter. Glue edges of circle into top of felt cylinder to form crown. Turn bottom edge of crown out ¼". Apply glue to underside and attach to brim.

Stuff hat lightly and glue or tack to head. Tie ribbon around hat to cover where band attaches to brim. Glue on holly decoration.

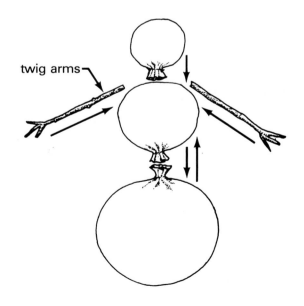

Figure—Assembly of Terry-Cloth Balls

twig arms

A VERSATILE CHRISTMAS QUILT

A popular early American quilt design, Drunkard's Path is ideal for the beginner. The design may appear complex, but it is actually created with two-piece blocks, assembled in four large squares. When made from festive calico fabrics, this traditional quilt becomes a lovely Christmas wall hanging, bed throw, or holiday table covering. If using the quilt as a tablecloth, protect it from spills by covering it with a clear plastic tablecloth.

YOU WILL NEED:
patterns on page 130
cardboard (for pattern template)
1¾ yd. (45"-wide) Christmas design fabric
¾ yd. (45"-wide) light-colored fabric
48" x 48" quilt batting
48" x 48" fabric for backing
1 yd. contrasting fabric (for binding)
thread to match

Prewash and iron all fabric. Transfer patterns to cardboard and cut out templates. On wrong side of fabric, and with straight lines parallel with grain of fabric, trace around templates 144 times each and cut out.

Lay out the two-piece blocks. Fold under ¼" along curved edges and iron. Pin pieces in place and stitch together. (Note: ¼" seam allowance.) Backstitch at the beginning and end of seams. (Do not knot.)

To assemble a 36-block square (Figure 1), first join blocks in each row, and then join rows. Repeat this procedure for 3 more 36-block squares. To form the quilt top, join the four squares as shown in the photograph. Iron the quilt top. Mark the quilting pattern (Figure 2) on quilt top with pencil or chalk.

Arrange quilt backing on a large flat surface and fasten corners with thumbtacks. Spread quilt batting evenly on backing. Lay quilt top over batting and smooth out. Baste the three layers together from center to edges and then around edges. (Figure 3).

Use a running stitch for outline quilting (Figure 2). Tie a knot in end of thread and bring needle through backing to top of quilt. Pull knot through backing and into batting so that it will not be seen. Start with center block and sew toward the edge. To finish, make a single backstitch and cut thread.

When quilting is completed, trim quilt edges. Cut bias strips 1"-wide and sew ends together to make one long strip. With right sides facing, lay bias strip along quilt edge. Sew through all thicknesses. Fold edge of bias strip under ¼". Fold strip to back of quilt and slip-stitch to backing.

Figure 1
36-Block Square

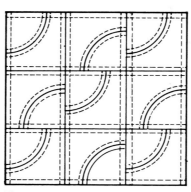

Figure 2
Mark quilting pattern on quilt top.

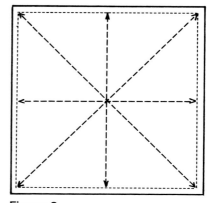

Figure 3
Baste layers together from center to edges.

PRESENT A PRETTY PAIR

These old-fashioned brother and sister dolls have identically embroidered faces. They stand eight inches tall and are made from a single body pattern. The frilly details of their fancy dress is very Victorian—a style influenced by the feminine and formal tastes of Victoria, Queen of England in the late 1800s and early 1900s.

YOU WILL NEED (for each doll):
patterns on page 147
9" x 12" flesh-colored cotton/polyester fabric (for body)
scraps of black fabric (for shoes)
pink, brown, flesh-colored embroidery floss
polyester stuffing
large darning needle

DOLL BODY: *Note:* Add ¼" seam allowance to all pattern pieces. To make the doll body, transfer pattern to back of fabric twice and cut out. Transfer shoe pattern to black fabric 4 times and cut out. With right sides facing, pin shoes to feet on both body pieces as shown in Figure 1. Sew shoes to feet where indicated on pattern. Fold shoes over feet and press. With right sides facing, sew body pieces together along seam line with a short machine stitch. Leave open where indicated on pattern. Clip curves, turn, and stuff. Slip-stitch opening closed.

To embroider face details, use 3 strands of floss. Make French knots for brown eyes and flesh-colored nose. Outline-stitch a pink mouth and brown eyebrows.

GIRL DOLL (hair and clothing):
¼ yd. white dotted-swiss fabric
3" x 8" white cotton/polyester fabric
½ yd. (½"-wide) white gathered lace
12" (⅛"-wide) red satin ribbon
12" (⅜"-wide) red satin ribbon
4½ yds. (4-ply) yellow knitting yarn (for hair)
small hat (optional)

To make hair, thread 2 yds. of yarn through a large darning needle and knot 1 end. Insert needle through back of doll's head and bring out at right side, along the dotted line shown on back of head (Figure 2). Satin-stitch between dotted lines at top and bottom of back of head until head is covered with vertical stitches. Make satin stitches on front of head from part (shown on pattern) to side seams. Keep stitches close together so that no fabric shows along the top of the head. Make a vertical stitch to cover the part. Push needle out through side of head, knot yarn, and cut.

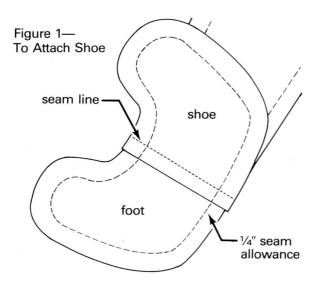

Figure 1—
To Attach Shoe

seam line

shoe

foot

¼" seam allowance

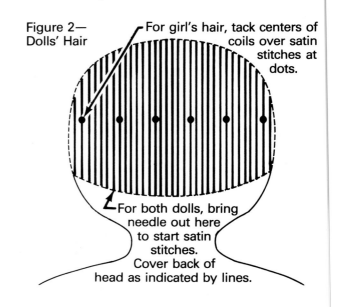

Figure 2—
Dolls' Hair

For girl's hair, tack centers of coils over satin stitches at dots.

For both dolls, bring needle out here to start satin stitches. Cover back of head as indicated by lines.

To make curls, wrap remaining yarn around a size 8 knitting needle or a couple of pencils. Stitch 1 loop to the next for entire length, remove from needle, and cut into 3″ coils. Tack center of each coil to back of head (Figure 2), with curls falling downward.

To dress girl doll, cut the bodice pattern from dotted-swiss fabric. For bodice back, cut center back where indicated on pattern. Stitch a small piece of gathered lace around neck edge. Hem sleeves and stitch lace along hemmed edges on wrong side. With right sides facing, stitch underarm and side seams of bodice.

For skirt, cut a 2½″ x 13″ rectangle from dotted-swiss fabric. Narrowly hem one long edge of the skirt. Make ¼″ pleats along long unhemmed edge. With right sides facing, stitch skirt to bodice. Stitch back seam to within 2″ of neck. Place dress on doll and slip-stitch back opening closed. Make a running stitch to gather sleeve edges, and pull to fit doll's arms. Tie ⅜″ ribbon at the waistline, make a bow, and tack at side of skirt. Tie ⅛″ ribbon around the neck, make a bow, and tack to neckline front.

Cut bloomers from white cotton/polyester fabric. With right sides facing, stitch side seams, stopping 1″ from waistline on one side. Sew lace along bottom of each leg. Stitch inside leg seams. Turn right side out. Hem top edge. Pull bloomers onto doll and stitch opening closed. Make a running stitch to gather leg edges and pull to fit legs.

BOY DOLL (hair and clothing):
3″ x 8″ black velvet fabric
6″ x 6″ white cotton/polyester fabric
½ yd. (½″-wide) white gathered lace
8″ (⅛″-wide) black ribbon
¼ yd. black bias tape
2 yds. (4-ply) brown knitting yarn (for hair)
1″ x 1″ basket (optional)

To make hair, thread 2 yds. yarn through a large darning needle and knot 1 end. Repeat girl's hair, omitting curls, and giving boy a side part as indicated on pattern.

To dress boy doll, cut shirt pattern from white cotton/polyester fabric. For shirt back, cut center back where indicated on pattern. According to pattern, stitch 4 rows of gathered lace to front of shirt. Stitch a row of lace around neck edge and at hemmed sleeve edges on wrong side. With right sides facing, stitch underarm and side seams. Put shirt on boy and stitch opening in back closed. Make a running stitch to gather sleeves, and pull to fit doll's arm. For suspenders, cut 4″ pieces of black ribbon. Tack to shirt in front, cross in back, and tack.

Cut knickers pattern from velvet fabric. With right sides facing, stitch side seams, stopping 1″ from waistline on one side. Sew black bias tape along bottom of each leg. Stitch inside leg seams. Turn right side out. Hem top edge. Pull knickers onto doll and stitch opening closed.

A FESTIVE FRAME OF MIND

Make holiday photos even more special with a Christmas frame. This colorful mat trimmed with holly and berries, and inserted in a plastic frame, stars Santa himself.

With a little help from you, children can create the artwork. Just transfer the patterns to watercolor paper, and let your child fill in the colors with paints or markers, as in a coloring book. Kids will enjoy the accomplishment as well as giving the frame as a gift to family and friends. For those who receive it—especially grandparents—it will be a treasure for years to come.

YOU WILL NEED:
pattern on page 146
5" x 7" acrylic frame
watercolor paper
watercolors or markers (red, green, light pink)
fine-point black marker
craft knife

Transfer pattern to watercolor paper. Fill in color on Santa and holly as shown in photograph. When dry, outline and add details in black. With a craft knife and on a protected surface, carefully cut out picture opening; then cut a 5" x 7" mat.

NOTEWORTHY NOTEPADS

If Christmas planning has you running in circles, take note. These quilted notepad covers are easy to make and will keep your important lists close at hand, so that you will be able to tell right away who's been naughty or nice.

The holidays bring numerous notes and lists of things to do—parties to attend, relatives arriving at different times, special foods to bake and last minute shopping—that make organization imperative. This year, add a festive touch to your planning with a quilted notepad cover, machine-stitched with one of these motifs.

Choose the size to fit your need—a notepad to carry in your purse, or one that stays next to the phone for messages during the busy holiday season. You could make a set for each of your busy friends. And because handmade gifts are special, your friends will enjoy receiving this practical as well as thoughtful gift.

YOU WILL NEED (for 5″ x 7″ pad):
patterns on page 136
¼ yd. cotton or cotton-blend fabric
¼ yd. fleece
1 package single-fold bias tape
contrasting thread
5″ x 7″ notepad

Cut 2 rectangles of fabric 16⅞″ x 5¾″. Place wrong sides together. Follow Figure to measure and mark spine lines. Stitch fabric together along these lines. Cut a 5¾″ x 6¾″

piece of fabric for a pocket. Set aside.

Cut a rectangle 8⅜″ x 5¾″ from fleece. Insert fleece between 2 pieces of front cover. Pin to hold in place and baste around outer edges through all layers. Center and transfer tree design to front of cover fabric. Machine-stitch along all lines.

Turn top edge of pocket ¼″ to wrong side and stitch to form a finished hem. Pin pocket face up to inside of back cover with corners aligned and hemmed edge toward spine.

Trim raw edges of cover ⅛″. Fold bias tape over raw edges and stitch to cover. Sew close to edge of tape as you go, making tiny folds at corners to finish edges. Insert cardboard back of notepad into pocket.

To make cover for 3″ x 4″ notepad, use the same assembly instructions as above, and change the dimensions as follows:

Cut 2 covers 3¼″ x 9⅜″. Position fabric as in Figure. Measurements for spine lines are 4⅝″ from front edge and 4½″ from back edge. Measurements for fleece lining are 3¼″ x 4⅝″. Pocket is 3¼″ x 4¼″. Center and transfer one of the leaf designs to the front of cover fabric. Machine-stitch along all lines.

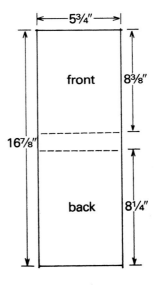

Figure—Dimensions for Measuring Spine Lines

QUILT-LOOK
WINTER VILLAGE

The piecing of prettily patterned fabrics gives this wall hanging the appearance of being quilted. But the quilt look is achieved without a needle and thread.

Simply score a foam block along all lines of the design, lay slightly oversized fabric cutouts over each section, and tuck edges into the scored lines. Choose fabrics to match a friend's favorite color scheme, or the curtains and pillows in a particular room.

YOU WILL NEED:
pattern on page 138
scraps of fabric (see pattern)
assorted scraps of ribbon and lace
15" x 12" x 1⅛" Styrofoam (craft foam)
cotton ball
pins with colored heads
straight pins

Enlarge the pattern and transfer to craft foam. With a butter knife, score craft foam ¼" deep along all lines. On back of craft foam, transfer and score border.

For each section of pattern, follow color chart for fabric. Adding ¼" to all pattern pieces, transfer to fabric and cut out. (It is better to cut fabric pieces too large than too small.) Lay fabric cutout over corresponding section on craft foam and push edges into scored lines. (Clip corners if necessary.) Use a small amount of glue to secure any fabric edges that will not stay.

For borders, cut fabric pieces—17" x 3½" for long sides, 11" x 3½" for short sides. On front, tuck long sides in place, then short sides. Turn craft foam over, bring fabric to back and tuck in place, folding corners neatly.

For chimney smoke, fluff and separate cotton ball and tuck into cracks above each chimney. For door knobs, insert colored-head pins into each door. Follow chart and photograph to trim village scene with ribbons and lace. Secure trim with straight pins.

A PLAYFUL PUPPY PILLOW

Frisky white puppies, playfully entangled in ribbon and surrounded by a border of ruffles, make a charming addition to a child's room. With embroidery stitches to make the eyes, nose, and mouth, you bring the puppy pillow to life. By using the contemporary colors shown, you are certain to find matching bedspreads or accent pieces. Or, choose your own colors to coordinate with an existing color scheme.

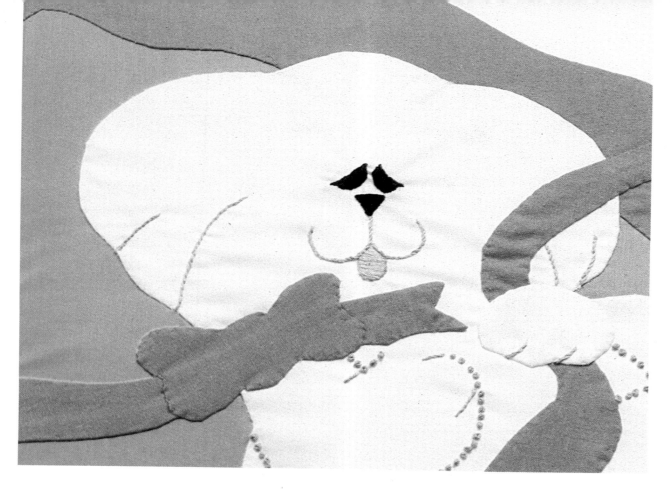

YOU WILL NEED:

patterns on page 140
1½ yds. (44"-wide) white polished cotton
½ yd. polished cotton for background
 (blue is shown)
¼ yd. polished cotton for bow, streamers,
 and borders (purple is shown)
embroidery floss (black, pink, gray)
16"-square pillow form

Follow the Figure to cut 2 (17"-square) pieces (for front and back of pillow) and 2 (9" x 54") ruffles from white polished cotton.

Assemble pattern. For background areas and borders, transfer outlines to fabric and cut out. Appliqué background to pillow front, turning edges under ¼" and clipping curves as necessary. Repeat for borders.

Mark outlines of puppies and embroidery details on white fabric. For embroidered details, use 2 strands of floss.

Cut out bodies for both puppies and pin in place. Appliqué the larger puppy first, then the smaller puppy. Cut streamers and appliqué in place; repeat for bows and paws.

To make the ruffle, sew ends, right sides together. Press seam open. Fold lengthwise, wrong sides together, and press. Make a running stitch along raw edges and gather. With right sides facing, pin ruffle to front of pillow, matching raw edges, and baste in place. Place pillow front to pillow back, right sides together, ruffle inside, and sew together, leaving one side open. Turn and press. Place pillow form inside and slip-stitch opening closed.

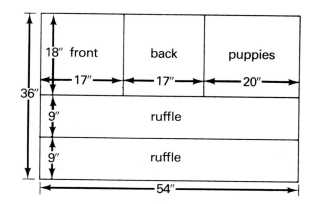

Figure—Fabric Cutting Layout

SPORTY SEASONAL SWEAT SUITS

Preparing for the holidays is a lot of work, but what fun! Gathering greenery, hanging garlands, stringing popcorn, trimming the tree. Get ready for all that light-hearted labor with brightly colored, cheerily trimmed sweat suits. You can't beat sweats for comfort, and with these timely trims, they're just right for Santa's helpers.

After you've decorated these store-bought separates for your family, you may want to share the idea, especially if you're in charge of organizing holiday activities for a group. For a caroling outing, deck all the songbirds in colorful uniforms. For a church or club bazaar, arrange an assembly line of member/workers to produce the outfits for sale at the fund-raiser. Then boost sales with the merry workers modeling their own creations.

Ideal as these clothes are for light work during the holidays, their sporty style makes them appropriate for many casual parties too—such as gatherings for ornament making or taffy pulling. Wear one of these jolly suits, and your appearance alone will set the scene for a festive time.

All you need to make these sweat suits are store-bought sweat clothes and small amounts of trim. The design application goes swiftly. For the wreath motif, twist strands of rickrack together in a circle and tack in place. Trim with a ribbon bow and machine-embroider red berries. For the snowman design, cut out the pattern from fabric scraps, iron in place with fusible fabric, and machine-appliqué around the outline. A ribbon forms the scarf. Facial details and random snowflakes are satin-stitched with embroidery floss. (Instructions are on the following page.)

SNOWMAN SWEAT SUIT:
patterns on page 149
⅛ yd. fabric (for snowmen)
Stitch Witchery (2-sided fusible fabric)
sweatshirt and sweatpants
1¼ yds. (⅜"-wide) red ribbon
white embroidery floss
thread to match
scraps of black fabric (for hat)

Cut out 4 snowmen (3 for shirt, 1 for pants) each from fabric and fusible fabric and pair. Position snowmen but do not fuse.

Cut four 11" lengths of ribbon for snowmen's scarves. For each scarf, cut 16 pieces of white floss into 2" lengths, fold in half, and sew 8 folded pieces of floss to each ribbon end for fringe. At snowmen's necks, place center of ribbon under fusible fabric. Press entire figure with iron. Machine satin-stitch outline of snowmen and tie ribbon in bows.

Cut out 4 hat patterns from black fabric and fusible fabric and pair. Arrange hats on snowmen, press in place, and satin-stitch outlines. Satin-stitch eyes, nose, and buttons in black. Satin-stitch mouth in red.

With three strands of white embroidery floss, embroider snowflakes at random around snowmen.

WREATH SWEATSHIRT:
medium green rickrack
sweatshirt
1½ yds. (¼"-wide) red ribbon
thread to match

To make a wreath, twist together two 8" strands of rickrack and pin ends to form a circle. Make 7 wreaths. Place wreaths on shirt and pin. Slip-stitch to shirt, catching each loop. Cut ribbon into 7" lengths and tie 7 bows. Tack bows to tops of wreaths. Machine-embroider 3 sets of 3 red berries on each wreath.

HAVE A COOL YULE!

Extend wishes for a cool Yule with this clever cross-stitch penguin box. The whimsical message combines with a bold, colorful design to fill this gift with offbeat fun.

The design is worked on 14-count Aida cloth. Then the box is trimmed with rows of textured ribbon.

For an element of surprise, hide another present inside. You could add to a prized collection, or tuck homemade sweets in pretty tissue.

YOU WILL NEED:
chart on page 148
8″ x 6½″ 14-count Aida cloth
embroidery floss
oval wooden Shaker box (6″ long)
8″ x 6½″ polyester fleece
craft glue
ribbon trims

Cross-stitch the design according to chart, using 4 strands of floss. (Outline in black with small, straight stitches using 1 strand floss.) Block finished stitchery.

Turn embroidered side down; turn box lid upside down, center on design, and trace around lid. Add ½″ to traced outline and cut oval. Every ½″ around edge, clip halfway to traced line. Trace around top of box lid on polyester fleece and cut out fleece.

Place fleece on wrong side of embroidery, aligning ovals. Apply a thin layer of glue to top and sides of box lid. Position lid upside down on fleece. Bring clipped edges of fabric up onto glued surface, smoothing them as you work.

Glue ribbon around sides of lid. Place lid on box and mark how far it comes down on box. Glue ribbon around box so that it meets lid.

Add rows of ribbon until box is covered from lid to bottom.

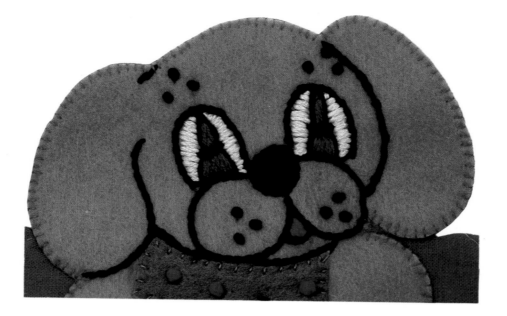

PERKY PET STOCKINGS

These cute pet stockings will hold a big Christmas ration of treats and toys. Reversible quilted fabric makes them easy to assemble, since it eliminates the need for lining. Heavyweight fusible fabric keeps the felt animal figures standing up pertly, and embroidered features add your own touch.

Choose felt the color of the pet's coat and match the shade of floss to its eyes. You can personalize the stocking even more by appliquéing or painting markings, such as spots for a dalmation or stripes for a tabby.

Pet stockings make adorable gifts alone, but try combining them with other gifts for added impact. If you're planning to give your child a puppy or kitten for Christmas, consider presenting the new pet in its very own stocking. Just leave the name tag blank and, once the pet is named, embroider the tag for future Christmases.

YOU WILL NEED (for two stockings):
patterns on page 144
¼ yd. reversible quilted fabric
9" squares of felt (for animal figures)
¼ yd. heavy-weight fusible fabric
embroidery floss (for colors, see pattern)

Transfer stocking and cuff patterns to fabric and cut out. Use opposite sides of reversible fabric for cuff and stocking. With right sides facing, sew stocking seam and trim. Turn right side out.

Sew side seams in cuff. Press seams open. Hem bottom of cuff. Slip cuff into stocking so that right side of cuff faces wrong side of stocking and unfinished top edges are even. Sew together, pull cuff out, and fold down over stocking.

For hanging loop, cut a 1" x 8" strip out of a scrap, press in half lengthwise, fold raw edges inside, and topstitch. Sew to top corner of stocking cuff.

To make cat or dog, iron fusible fabric to a 9" square of felt in body color. Transfer the animal pattern to felt—once with detail for front, and once (reversing pattern) in outline only for back. Embroider design according to pattern and photo, using 3 strands of floss doubled and knotted.

Cut the collar out of contrasting felt and sew to animal with a blanket stitch. Cut out both animal outlines and sew wrong sides together with blanket stitch. Place animal on top edge of cuff and sew in place.

For tags, iron fusible fabric to felt. Transfer pattern and cut out. Embroider your pet's name and attach to cuff with blanket stitch. Connect tag to collar with a loop of floss. For the cat's Christmas bow, cut a ½"-wide strip of green felt, tie in a bow, and tack to collar.

A CHORUS OF CAROLERS

Simple wooden cutouts and easy-to-follow painting instructions make these Victorian carolers, who will stay in mid-song throughout the holidays.

In nineteenth century England, after a rousing chorus of a favorite carol, the singers would be invited into the family's home, to warm themselves by the fire with a mug of wassail or syllabub.

The long skirts, fur muffs and top hats shown on the carolers are typical costumes of that day. Subtle shading gives depth to their outfits. A dry-brush technique achieves the subdued plaid design on the women's skirts.

Although shown in a window, this chorus of carolers could be used on a buffet, or to decorate a mantel.

YOU WILL NEED (for 4 carolers):
patterns on page 137
12" of 1" x 12" white pine
jigsaw or band saw
sandpaper
wood sealer
acrylic paints (red, black, flesh, green)
brushes
water-based varnish

Transfer pattern outlines to wood and cut out. Sand and apply a coat of sealer. Transfer pattern details to cutout (or paint freehand if desired). Paint back and edges as patterns indicate. Let dry. Paint front following photo. Let dry. Apply coat of varnish. Let dry thoroughly.

MR. CLOWN
MAKES IT ALL BETTER

When children get an accidental bruise or scrape, chase away the tears with an icepack clown. Just slip in a couple of ice cubes and hold Mr. Clown on the bump. His machine-embroidered smile should perk up even the saddest little face.

Lined with vinyl, these terry cloth icepacks are washable, too, making them ready for many answers to the call of duty.

Stitch a few icepack stocking stuffers for young friends. Chances are, they'll find these icepacks as much fun to play with as they are comforting.

YOU WILL NEED:
patterns on page 150
scraps of terry cloth and assorted prints
lightweight vinyl
thread (for machine-stitched face details)
yarn (for hair)
pom-pom

Cut 1 face from terry cloth, 2 hats from 1 calico print, and 2 back sections from another print. For a waterproof liner, cut 1 face and 2 back sections from vinyl.

Transfer features to the terry cloth face. From calico, cut a small circle for a nose, and 2 triangular eyes. Satin-stitch nose and eyes to face. Satin-stitch mouth with red thread. Cut 3" lengths of yarn for hair and fold in half. With loops toward inside of face, place yarn ends between x's even with edge of face, and baste (Figure 1).

Baste vinyl to wrong sides of back sections and clown face. Fold straight edge of each back section over liner and hem. Pin both back sections to the clown face, right sides facing (Figure 2). (The yarn loops will be inside.) Sew all thicknesses together. Clip the seam, turn, and press.

For hat, sew pieces together with right sides facing, leaving the bottom edge open. Turn hat and fold bottom ¼" toward inside. Place hat on head, and slip-stitch in place. Tack a pom-pom to the point of the hat.

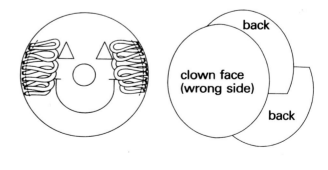

Figure 1
To Attach Yarn Hair

Figure 2
Assembly of Icepack

STARRY NIGHT AFGHAN

Stars in the winter sky are echoed in cross-stitch on this cozy afghan. Whoever receives it will be warmed by the hours of affection that went into its making.

The technique used here is Tunisian crochet, or afghan stitch, which creates a firm knit-like fabric. Its stitches actually form a grid for the cross-stitch.

This piece is crocheted using an afghan hook, which has a knob on one end to keep stitches from sliding off. Rows are worked leaving all stitches on the hook and moving back and forth without turning the work.

It's extremely important to block the piece when finished. Since this fabric tends to pull on the bias, be careful to keep the afghan square during blocking.

YOU WILL NEED:
#10 afghan crochet hook
8 skeins (3½ oz.) royal blue knitting worsted yarn
12 skeins (1.4 oz.) 3-ply white mohair-look yarn
yarn needle (for cross-stitch)

GAUGE: Ch 40 = 10″, 30 rows = 10″.

SQUARES: With blue yarn, ch 40. *Row 1:* Sk 1 ch, * insert hook in next ch, draw up a loop *. *Row 2:* Yo, draw through 1 loop, * yo, draw through 2 loops *. *Row 3:* Ch 1, * insert hook right to left under next vertical st, draw up a loop *. Repeat from Row 2 until there are 30 rows. Tie off. This makes one square. Repeat to make 20 squares.

BORDER: Working with 2 strands of white yarn at once, tie onto corner of blue square. *Row 1:* Ch 2, sc in same sp as joining, (sc in each sp to corner, 2 sc in next sp) 3 times. Sc in each sp to corner, sl st in top of beginning ch 2. *Row 2:* Ch 1, 2 sc in next sc, (sc in each sc to corner, 3 sc in corner) 3 times. Sc in each sc to corner, sl st in ch 1, tie off.

CROSS-STITCH: Use 2 strands of white floss to work cross-stitch, as shown in photo. Hide thread on back of work by running needle under afghan stitches. Tie off thread at each cross.

JOINING: Use 2 strands of white yarn and a yarn needle to join squares with an overcast stitch. Refer to Figure for assembly of squares.

FINISHING: Tie on 2 strands of white at one corner. Ch 2, sc in each sc around entire afghan. Sl st to beginning ch 2. Tie off.

Standard Crochet Abbreviations

ch - chain	**sc** - single crochet
sk - skip	**sp** - space
yo - yarn over	**sl st** - slip stitch
st - stitch	

* * Instructions between asterisks should be repeated as many times as there are stitches to accommodate them.

( ) A series of steps within parentheses should be worked according to instructions that follow the parentheses.

	x x x x x x x x x		x x x x x x x x x	
x x x x x x x x x		x x x x x x x x x		x x x x x x x x x
	x x x x x x x x x		x x x x x x x x x	
x x x x x x x x x		x x x x x x x x x		x x x x x x x x x

Figure—Assembly of Squares

RUFFLES AND LACE: A COUNTRY HEART

Ribbons and lace and bright plaid fabric cover craft foam and cotton balls, to make a puffy heart that's a dainty accent piece.

This pretty decoration might be just the thing to brighten a special spot during the holidays, but it doesn't have to come down with the tree ornaments. By choosing your materials with a friend's home in mind, this heart can work through all the seasons.

Here, broadcloth and cotton make the heart a charming example of the popular country look. But if your friend has an elegant, romantic bedroom, you might want to use satin ribbon, moiré taffeta, and a few silk rosebuds.

YOU WILL NEED:
patterns on page 149
24" x 12" (1"-thick) Styrofoam (craft foam) sheet
2 yds. (36"-wide) fabric
craft glue
85" (2"-wide) lace
thread to match
35 large cotton balls
florist's pins (1¾", U-shaped)

To make the large heart, transfer large heart pattern to craft foam and cut out. On the fabric, sketch a heart 3" larger than the craft foam heart and cut out.

Place craft foam heart on the wrong side of fabric. Pull fabric up over the edges of the craft foam heart and glue along the edge of front (Figure 1). Be sure the fabric on the back is pulled smooth. Let glue dry. (Note: When gluing lace or fabric to craft foam, pin to secure while drying.)

Cut 45" of lace. Make a long running stitch along edge and gather to fit around edge of large heart. Glue lace on fabric along edge of heart so that 1½" of lace extends beyond edge (Figure 2).

To make the small heart, transfer small heart pattern to craft foam and cut out. Glue small heart to center front of larger heart (Figure 2).

To make the ruffle, cut a strip of fabric 5" x 85". Fold fabric in half lengthwise, wrong sides facing, and baste raw edges together. Gather ruffle to fit and glue to the front of large heart, edges against small heart (Figure 2). Gather remaining lace to fit around sides of small heart and glue (Figure 3).

Cut 35 four-inch fabric circles. Place a large cotton ball in center of fabric circle and twist edges of circle together to form a puff. With florist's pins, attach a row of puffs around front edge of small heart (Figure 3). Fill in with remaining puffs. Small bows, lace, baby's breath, or silk flowers can be attached with florist's pins to decorate or hide any gaps left between puffs. To hang, attach a ribbon loop to back of heart with glue.

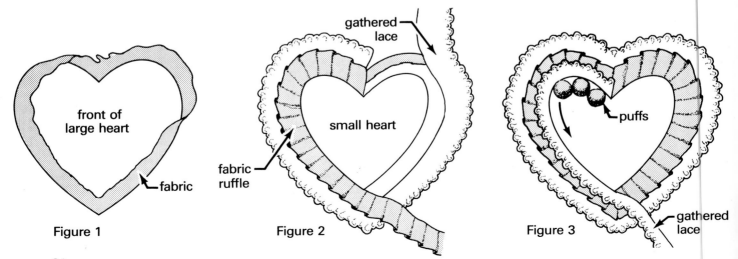

front of large heart — fabric

Figure 1

gathered lace — fabric ruffle — small heart

Figure 2

puffs — gathered lace

Figure 3

APPLIQUÉ WITH CHRISTMAS CUTOUTS

Colorful cutouts and fusible fabric make this no-stitch appliqué table runner quick to put together. You can make several for gifts and still have time to include one for yourself this Christmas. The edges of the runner are finished with quilt binding. Then trees and bows are cut out and attached, using fusible fabric.

The runner shown here is made with broadcloth and country calico, but other fabrics can be chosen to match dishes, furnishings, or special decorations. For a nice extra touch, appliqué matching napkins by using just the bow design.

It might be wise to use a spray fabric protector to help prevent staining. Make sure the fabrics are compatible with the spray, by following the manufacturer's directions for testing on fabric scraps, before treating the runner itself.

YOU WILL NEED:
patterns on page 150
⅔ yd. (45"-wide) white broadcloth
¼ yd. green broadcloth
¼ yd. red calico
½ yd. Stitch Witchery (2-sided fusible fabric)
2 packages red double-fold quilt binding

Cut a 20" x 42" rectangle from white fabric. Sew quilt binding to edges of rectangle, mitering corners neatly. Cut tree patterns from green broadcloth and fusible fabric, and pair. Repeat for bow patterns.

To position trees for appliqué, mark center point of short edge of runner. Center a tree 2" from bottom edge. Place a tree ¾" on either side of first tree. Repeat on opposite end.

Make a dot 2" above each tree and center a bow over each dot. To fuse, iron trees and bows to runner, following manufacturer's directions. Then turn runner over and iron.

QUICK-WEAVE PLACE MATS

With the two quick-weave techniques featured here, you can make sets of place mats for last-minute gift giving or decorating. Just weave rickrack and bias tape through needlepoint canvas or ribbon through Aida cloth, and you have festive additions for the holiday table.

RIBBON-EMBROIDERED MAT (for 1 mat):
chart on page 151
12" x 17½" piece green 11-count Aida fabric
masking tape
4½ yards (⅛"-wide) white satin ribbon
large-eyed tapestry needle
craft glue

To prevent raveling of fabric, tape edges with masking tape. From ribbon, cut four 17" lengths and four 11" lengths for borders. Cut twenty 4" lengths for snowflakes.

Beginning at the lower left corner of the place mat, count up 13 squares and over 13 squares. With tapestry needle, thread ribbon from back to front through this hole.

From left to right, darn over 11 squares, under 1, over 11 squares and under 1, until you have 14 long stitches on the top of the mat. Pull ribbon ends to the back and glue ends to the back of the mat. Count 2 squares above row just worked and repeat pattern for a second row of ribbon. Repeat for opposite side of mat.

On a short side, begin at the lower left corner, and count up 12 squares and over 12 squares. Thread ribbon from back to front through this opening. Weave same pattern as above for 9 long stitches. Repeat for opposite side of mat. Pull ribbon ends to the back and glue ends to mat.

For snowflakes, begin in lower right corner of mat where inside rows of ribbon form a corner, and count 2 squares over and 2 squares up to begin the snowflake. (See Chart.) After working each line of stitches, pull ends to back, trim, and glue. Repeat for top left corner.

To fringe the mat edges, remove tape and unravel the first 3 rows of thread all around mat.

WOVEN CANVAS MATS (for 2 mats):
chart on page 151
½ yd. (#5 mesh) white polyester needlepoint canvas
craft glue
1 package (medium-width) red rickrack
masking tape
1 package each (⅜"-wide) red and green
   bias tape

Measure a 61-mesh x 81-mesh rectangle
(62 threads x 82 threads) on the canvas. To
prevent raveling, add ⅛" on all sides and cut
out rectangle. Run a bead of glue along the
first and 62nd horizontal threads and the first
and 82nd vertical threads. Allow to dry thoroughly.

Fold end of rickrack to a point and tape
with masking tape to make weaving easier.
To find starting point, begin at lower left corner of mat and count up 3 squares, then
over 3 squares. Mark this square lightly with
a pencil. Thread rickrack through opening
from back to front.

Following the chart, weave rickrack along
the bottom edge over unmarked threads and
under threads marked by a dot. Continue
around the mat, returning to starting point.
Trim ends of rickrack and glue together on
underside of mat.

To prepare for weaving bias tape, slots
must be cut in the canvas. To make a slot 2
squares wide, cut away the thread between
the 2 adjacent squares indicated on the
chart.

Prepare end of bias tape for weaving as
with rickrack. Following chart, thread green
tape from back to front through slot in bottom left corner and weave across the bottom
edge. At each corner, pull bias tape to underside and cut, leaving 1" tape at each end.
Repeat for all sides. At corners, fold together
tape ends from adjacent sides. Trim and glue
on underside to secure.

Inside the border of green tape, weave a
border of red tape and then a second border
of green tape. To complete the mat, trim
ends of yarn around edges.

AN ANGEL OF AN APRON

This elegant apron is made with net darning—a fundamental, over/under weaving technique. The beautiful results approximate those of the time-consuming art of filet lace making.

Filet lace makers construct their own net and create designs in it by elaborately weaving thread through the squares.

This apron offers the same effect, but in a fraction of the time. And, thanks to washable modern fibers, the results are as practical as they are lovely.

YOU WILL NEED:
charts on page 151
24" x 40" white net (6 squares per inch)
100 yds. ecru #3 mercerized thread
#16 tapestry needle
2 yds. (2"-wide) red washable satin ribbon

Choose net that will not shrink or require a hoop, if possible. If not, wash and block net before beginning this project.

Remove selvage (finished edge) from net. Turn 5 rows under on short side of net. Leaving 3" excess thread in back of net, darn the 2 layers of net together through first, third, and fifth rows with a continuous length of thread. Knot ends and run excess thread back into the same row of squares. Repeat for other short side and for 1 long side (this is hem of apron).

For top of apron, fold under 15 squares. Darn twice along raw edge through the same row of squares to make double lines of stitches. Count down 6 squares from top, and in that row work double lines of stitches. Large opening will be a casing for the ribbon tie.

TREES: Each tree is 16 squares tall. Apron contains 11 trees, with trunks spaced 20 squares apart. Fold apron in half to find center square. Start one row above last line of stitches at bottom hem and stitch center tree following chart. Darn across 20 squares to the left and repeat for 5 trees. When left side is finished, return to center tree, stitch over 20 spaces and begin trees for right side.

ANGELS: Follow chart to position angel with trumpet, so that right edge of angel is about 6½" from right side of apron and lowest point of angel is about 6½" from bottom of apron. Beginning at angel's forehead, darn back and forth horizontally through each row of squares to open spaces in chart, being careful not to fill in open spaces. Weave until squares are filled—3 or 4 threads in most cases (Figure). To finish, weave about ¾" of thread vertically between lines of stitches on reverse side and cut excess close to net. Repeat process on other side of apron, using angel with lyre chart.

STARS: Follow chart and place stars in sky as desired.

FINISHING: Thread ribbon through casing for tie.

Figure—Weaving
Weave back and forth to fill squares—3 or 4 threads in most cases.

YOUR CHRISTMAS KITCHEN

The heart of the home is the kitchen, especially at Christmastime. What transpires there—licking the beaters, breathing in the heady warmth and aroma, savoring the first bite hot from the oven—is the stuff of memories. Try the following recipes and start some memories of your own.

GIFTS OF HOME COOKING

COOKIE GIFT BOXES
GERMAN STOLLEN
ALMOND CREME LIQUEUR
BUTTERSCOTCH POPCORN BARK
SAVORY CORNMEAL THINS
HOMEMADE MAPLE SYRUP
COFFEE ALMOND PRALINE TOPPING
MARMALADE MERINGUE BARS
RAISIN SAUCE
HONEYED FIGS
SWISS ALMOND TEA WAFERS
HOT BUTTERED DRINK MIX
CHERRY WINKS
GRANOLA SNACK MIX

Gifts from the kitchen are a joy in the making as well as the giving. The time spent in preparing is a period of happy reflection. And for the person who receives your home-made gift of food, the treat will be extra enjoyable because you made it.

From these recipes, tailor food gifts to individual tastes. Candies will gratify a sweet tooth, and cookies will appease the cookie monster. Treats with fruit, nuts, and grains will convince a health food fan, while syrups and sauces will provide variety for ice cream aficionados.

COOKIE GIFT BOXES
Molasses Cookie Dough
Melted sugar (recipe follows)
Royal Icing
Paste food coloring

Share homemade treats with friends. Clockwise from bottom right: Butterscotch Popcorn Bark, Swiss Almond Tea Wafers, Almond Creme Liqueur, German Stollen, and Cookie Gift Boxes filled with Savory Cornmeal Thins, Granola Snack Mix, and more Butterscotch Popcorn Bark.

Cut the following shapes from cardboard to make patterns for boxes: 1 (3¾ x 2½-inch) rectangle for bottom; 2 (3¾ x 1½-inch) rectangles and 2 (2¾ x 1½-inch) rectangles for sides; and 1 (4 x 3-inch) rectangle for lid. Set aside. Grease and flour 2 large cookie sheets.

Divide Molasses Cookie Dough into 2 equal portions. Roll each portion of dough to cover a prepared cookie sheet, rolling dough to ¼-inch thickness. Arrange patterns on one dough-filled cookie sheet, spacing patterns ½-inch apart; cut around patterns using the tip of a sharp knife. Remove excess dough, reserving for rerolling. Remove patterns, and arrange on second dough-filled cookie sheet; repeat trimming procedure. Bake cookies at 325° for 20 to 25 minutes or until firm and golden brown (reverse cookie sheets on oven racks after 15 minutes for more even browning). Remove from cookie sheets, and cool completely on wire racks. Reroll scraps of dough onto 2 greased and floured cookie sheets; repeat tracing and trimming procedures to make parts for 2 additional cookie boxes. Bake and cool as directed.

Prepare melted sugar. To assemble cookie gift box, place a bottom cookie rectangle, top side up, on a board covered with greased waxed paper. Dip one long edge and 2 side edges of a cookie rectangle side into melted sugar; press onto long edge of box bottom, and hold in place until set (about 2 seconds). (Work quickly when dipping; melted sugar hardens quickly. Be careful not to touch sugar; it is very hot.) Repeat with 3 other cookie rectangle sides, dipping edges into melted sugar, and holding in place on corresponding edge of box bottom. Repeat procedure with remaining cookie pieces and melted sugar to make 3 additional boxes.

Place small amounts of Royal Icing into separate bowls for each color desired; color with paste food coloring. Pipe desired trim on boxes using No. 16 fluted tip for borders, No. 67 leaf tip for leaves, and No. 2 or 3 round tip for berries. Let dry overnight. Fill cookie gift boxes with cookies or candy; top each with lid, and tie together with ribbon, if desired. Store in airtight container up to 1 month. Yield: 4 cookie gift boxes.

Molasses Cookie Dough:
1 cup molasses
3 tablespoons butter or margarine, melted
1 egg, beaten
½ teaspoon baking soda
1 teaspoon ground allspice
¼ teaspoon ground nutmeg
3½ to 4 cups all-purpose flour, divided

Combine first 6 ingredients in a large bowl; mix well. Gradually add 2½ cups flour to molasses mixture, stirring well. Knead in enough remaining flour to make a stiff dough. Gather dough into a ball. Yield: enough dough to make 4 cookie gift boxes.

Melted Sugar:
½ cup sugar

Place ½ cup sugar in a small, heavy saucepan; cook over medium heat, stirring constantly, until syrupy and caramel-colored. Reduce heat to low, and let saucepan remain on heat to keep sugar from hardening. Use quickly before sugar browns too much. (Be careful not to touch syrup with hands. It is very hot.) Yield: enough to make 4 cookie gift boxes.

Royal Icing:
3 egg whites
½ teaspoon cream of tartar
1 (16-ounce) package powdered sugar

Combine egg whites (at room temperature) and cream of tartar in a large mixing bowl. Beat at high speed of an electric mixer until frothy. Add half of powdered sugar, mixing well. Add remaining sugar, and beat 5 to 7 minutes at high speed. Yield: about 2 cups.

Note: Royal Icing dries very quickly; keep covered at all times with a damp cloth. Do not double this recipe. If additional icing is needed, prepare another batch.

GERMAN STOLLEN
1 package dry yeast
¼ cup warm water (105° to 115°)
½ cup butter, softened
¼ cup sugar
1 teaspoon salt
2 eggs
1 cup milk, scalded and cooled to lukewarm
4½ cups all-purpose flour
½ cup chopped almonds
½ cup coarsely chopped candied red and green cherries
½ cup raisins
1 cup sifted powdered sugar (optional)
2 tablespoons hot water (optional)
Sliced almonds (optional)
Red and green candied cherry halves (optional)

Dissolve yeast in warm water; let stand 5 minutes.

Cream butter, sugar, and salt in a large bowl until light and fluffy. Add eggs, one at a time, beating well after each addition. Stir in milk and yeast mixture. Add flour, 1 cup at a time, stirring well, until a soft dough is formed. Cover tightly, and let rise in a warm place (85°), free from drafts, 1½ hours or until doubled in bulk.

Punch dough down. Knead almonds, candied cherries, and raisins into dough on a lightly floured surface. Divide dough in half. Roll each half to a 10-inch circle; fold in half, and place on a greased baking sheet. Let loaves rise in a warm place, free from drafts, 30 minutes or until doubled in bulk.

Bake loaves at 375° for 25 to 30 minutes or until golden brown; loaves will sound hollow when tapped on top with finger. Cool on wire racks 2 to 3 minutes.

If glaze is desired, combine powdered sugar and hot water; spread over each loaf. Garnish with sliced almonds and candied cherries, if desired. Store in airtight container up to 2 days. Yield: 2 loaves.

ALMOND CREME LIQUEUR

1 (14-ounce) can sweetened condensed
  milk
1¾ cups amaretto
1 cup whipping cream
4 eggs
1 teaspoon instant coffee powder
2 teaspoons almond extract
2 teaspoons vanilla extract

Combine all ingredients in container of an electric blender; process until blended. Store in a tightly closed jar in refrigerator for up to 1 month. Serve chilled; stir before serving. Yield: 4⅓ cups.

BUTTERSCOTCH POPCORN BARK

3 (6-ounce) packages butterscotch morsels
½ teaspoon ground cinnamon
2 cups popped corn
1 cup whole blanched almonds, toasted
1 (6-ounce) package semisweet chocolate
  morsels

Place butterscotch morsels in a large glass bowl; microwave at HIGH for 3 minutes. Add cinnamon, and stir until smooth. Add popped corn and almonds, stirring to coat well. Spread mixture evenly into a 12 x 8-inch rectangle on a lightly oiled baking sheet; refrigerate 30 minutes or until firm.

Place chocolate morsels in a small glass bowl; microwave at HIGH for 2 minutes. Stir until smooth. Pipe or drizzle chocolate in a lacy pattern over candy; refrigerate 15 minutes or until set. Break into pieces using a knife. Store in airtight container up to 1 week. Yield: ¾ pound.

SAVORY CORNMEAL THINS

1¾ cups self-rising flour
¾ cup plain yellow cornmeal
2 tablespoons sugar
½ cup butter or margarine, frozen and
  cut into pieces
2 tablespoons vinegar
2 tablespoons dry sherry (optional)
3 to 4 tablespoons ice water
¼ cup butter or margarine, melted
Grated Parmesan cheese or poppy seeds

Position knife blade in food processor bowl. Add flour, cornmeal, and sugar; top with cover. Process 5 seconds or until blended. Add butter; process, using start/stop technique, just until mixture forms coarse crumbs. With processor running, slowly pour vinegar and sherry through food chute; gradually add just enough water in a slow, steady stream to make dough form a ball.

Divide dough into 2 equal portions; roll out each portion to ¹⁄₁₆-inch thickness on an ungreased baking sheet. Cut into rounds using a 2-inch biscuit cutter, spacing ½-inch

apart; remove scraps, and reserve for rerolling. Brush tops of rounds lightly with melted butter; sprinkle lightly with Parmesan cheese. Bake at 375° for 10 minutes or until lightly browned. Cool on wire racks; store in airtight containers up to 1 week. Yield: 7 dozen.

HOMEMADE MAPLE SYRUP

1 cup water
2 cups sugar
½ teaspoon maple flavoring
½ cup chopped walnuts

Bring water to a boil in a 1-quart saucepan; add sugar, maple flavoring, and walnuts, stirring to dissolve. Cook 1 to 2 minutes, stirring constantly. Remove from heat. Chill. Store in refrigerator up to 1 month. Yield: 2 cups.

COFFEE ALMOND PRALINE TOPPING

1½ cups whole blanched almonds
Vegetable cooking spray
1½ cups sugar
½ cup strong brewed coffee
½ teaspoon cream of tartar

Place almonds in a single layer in a shallow baking dish; bake at 350° for 20 minutes or until golden brown. Shake pan occasionally to stir the almonds; cool.

Line a jellyroll pan with aluminum foil; coat foil with cooking spray, and set aside.

Coat a heavy, 2-quart saucepan with cooking spray; combine sugar, coffee, and cream of tartar in saucepan. Cook over medium-high heat, stirring constantly with a wooden spoon, until sugar dissolves. Wash down sides of saucepan with a pastry brush dipped in cold water to remove undissolved sugar granules. Boil, without stirring, for 6 to 8 minutes or until syrup turns a dark caramel color. (Watch carefully to make sure syrup does not boil over. Lift the pan occasionally, and swirl it slightly to "stir" the syrup.) Coat a wooden spoon with cooking spray. Add almonds to syrup, and stir quickly to coat well. Pour mixture in a thin layer on prepared pan; cool completely.

Peel foil from back of cooled praline; break praline into pieces. Process praline, in batches, in a blender or food processor until ground. Store in airtight containers (or praline will absorb moisture and become sticky) in the refrigerator for 1 week. Sprinkle over ice cream, cake frosting, pies, or fruit desserts just before serving. Yield: 3 cups.

MARMALADE MERINGUE BARS
¼ cup plus 2 tablespoons butter or
  margarine, softened
½ cup sugar, divided
2 eggs, separated
1 teaspoon grated orange rind
1 teaspoon vanilla extract
1 cup all-purpose flour
½ cup wheat germ, toasted and divided
½ cup finely chopped pecans, divided
¼ teaspoon salt
⅓ cup orange marmalade
Sifted powdered sugar

Cream butter in a medium-size mixing bowl; gradually add ¼ cup sugar, beating until light and fluffy. Beat in egg yolks, orange rind, and vanilla. Combine flour, ¼ cup wheat germ, ¼ cup pecans, and salt; add to creamed mixture, mixing well. Press dough evenly on bottom and 1 inch up sides of an ungreased 8-inch square baking pan. Bake at 350° for 12 to 15 minutes or until golden brown.

Beat egg whites (at room temperature) until soft peaks form; gradually add remaining ¼ cup sugar, 1 tablespoon at a time, beating until stiff peaks form. Fold in remaining ¼ cup wheat germ and ¼ cup pecans; set aside.

Spread marmalade over hot pastry; top with meringue mixture. Bake at 350° for 18 to 20 minutes or until golden brown. Cool on wire rack. Sprinkle with powdered sugar; cut into bars. Store in airtight container up to 1 week. Yield: 2 dozen.

RAISIN SAUCE
1 cup sugar
½ cup water
1 cup raisins
2 tablespoons butter or margarine
2 tablespoons vinegar
Dash of Worcestershire sauce
½ teaspoon salt
¼ teaspoon ground cloves
2 teaspoons cornstarch

Combine all ingredients except cornstarch; bring to a boil. Cook until raisins are plump. Dissolve cornstarch in a small amount of cold water; gradually add to hot mixture. Cook until clear, stirring constantly. Chill until serving time or up to 2 weeks. Serve over cooked meats. Yield: about 2 cups.

HONEYED FIGS
6 cups dried figs
12 cups water
2½ cups honey
2 cups sugar
⅔ cup port wine
⅓ cup lemon juice
½ teaspoon whole cloves
2 lemons, thinly sliced

Combine figs and water in a large Dutch oven; bring to a boil. Cover, reduce heat, and simmer 1 hour or until figs are tender. Remove from heat, and let stand at room temperature overnight. Drain figs, reserving 1 cup liquid.

Combine fig liquid, honey, sugar, wine, lemon juice, and cloves in a Dutch oven; cook over medium heat, stirring constantly, until sugar dissolves. Add figs; bring to a boil, and cook, uncovered, 10 minutes, stirring occasionally. Add lemon slices, and boil 15 minutes. Remove figs using a slotted spoon, and set aside; bring syrup to a boil, and cook an additional 15 minutes over medium heat. Return figs to syrup; skim off foam using a metal spoon.

Quickly ladle figs and liquid into hot jars, leaving ¼-inch headspace; cover at once with metal lids, and screw bands tight. Process in boiling-water bath 20 minutes. Serve with smoked turkey, cured meats, pork, or duck; or serve as a topping for ice cream or waffles. Store in cool, dry place up to 1 year. Yield: 7 to 8 half-pints.

SWISS ALMOND TEA WAFERS

1½ cups sliced almonds, lightly toasted
½ cup sugar
2 teaspoons grated orange rind
½ cup butter or margarine, softened
1 egg
2 egg yolks
2 tablespoons amaretto
2¼ cups all-purpose flour
¼ teaspoon salt
1 egg yolk
1 tablespoon water
About 2 tablespoons sugar
Silver candy decorations

Combine almonds, ½ cup sugar, and orange rind in container of a food processor or electric blender; process until finely ground.

Cream butter; add almond mixture, beating well. Add next 3 ingredients; beat well. Combine flour and salt; add to creamed mixture, and blend well. Shape dough into a ball; wrap, and chill until firm.

Roll dough to ¼-inch thickness between 2 sheets of waxed paper. (Turn dough over and loosen paper every 2 or 3 rolls to allow dough to spread.) Cut dough using a 2-inch cutter, rerolling scraps of dough.

Place cookies ½-inch apart on greased and floured baking sheets. Combine 1 egg yolk and water; brush over cookies. Sprinkle cookies lightly with sugar, and decorate as desired with candy decorations. Bake at 350° for 15 to 18 minutes or until cookies are browned around edges and golden in center. Cool on racks; store in airtight containers for 1 week. Yield: about 5½ dozen.

HOT BUTTERED DRINK MIX

2 cups butter, softened
4 cups firmly packed light brown sugar
1 tablespoon plus 2 teaspoons pumpkin
  pie spice
2 teaspoons ground cinnamon
1 teaspoon vanilla extract

Cream butter in a large mixing bowl; gradually add sugar and spices, and beat until smooth at high speed of an electric mixer. Stir in vanilla. Store in airtight containers for 1 month in refrigerator or 3 months in freezer. Include following recipes with gift package. Yield: 4½ cups mix.

Rum Toddy:

1 cup boiling water
2 tablespoons rum
1 tablespoon Hot Buttered Drink Mix
1 (4-inch) stick cinnamon (optional)

Combine the boiling water, the rum, and the Hot Drink Mix in a mug; stir well. Garnish with cinnamon stick, if desired. Yield: 1 cup.

Mulled Cider:

1 cup boiling apple cider or juice
1 tablespoon Hot Buttered Drink Mix
1 orange slice (optional)
Freshly grated nutmeg (optional)

Combine the apple cider and the Hot Drink Mix in a mug; stir well. Garnish with orange slice, and sprinkle with nutmeg, if desired. Yield: 1 cup.

Café au Lait:

½ cup hot milk
½ cup strong hot coffee
1 tablespoon Hot Buttered Drink Mix
Whipped cream (optional)
Grated chocolate (optional)

Combine first 3 ingredients in a mug; stir well. Garnish with a dollop of whipped cream, and sprinkle with chocolate, if desired. Yield: 1 cup.

CHERRY WINKS

1 cup shortening
1 (3-ounce) package cream cheese,
  softened
1 cup sugar
1 egg
1 teaspoon almond extract
2½ cups all-purpose flour
¼ teaspoon baking soda
½ teaspoon salt
1¼ cups finely chopped pecans
36 maraschino cherries, halved

Cream shortening and cream cheese; gradually add sugar, beating until light and fluffy. Add egg and almond extract; beat well.
Combine flour, soda, and salt; add to creamed mixture, beating well. Chill about 1 hour.
Shape dough into 1-inch balls; roll in pecans. Place on ungreased baking sheets; press a cherry half into the center of each cookie. Bake at 350° for 12 to 15 minutes. Store in airtight container in refrigerator up to 1 week. Yield: about 6 dozen.

GRANOLA SNACK MIX

1½ cups regular oats, uncooked
1 cup coarsely chopped walnuts
1 cup flaked coconut
1 cup sunflower kernels
½ teaspoon apple or pumpkin pie spice
½ cup butter-flavored syrup
1 cup carob-coated raisins
1 cup banana chips (optional)

Combine first 5 ingredients; mix well. Pour syrup over oats mixture; stirring well. Spread mixture in a single layer on a lightly greased jellyroll pan. Bake at 300° for 1 hour, stirring every 15 minutes. Then cool completely.
Add carob-coated raisins and banana chips to cooled mixture; store in airtight containers up to 2 weeks. Yield: 5½ cups.

ELEGANT DESSERTS

RASPBERRY TART
LIME CREAM DESSERT
CHOCOLATE ORANGE MERINGUE TORTE
WHITE APRICOT-GLAZED FRUITCAKE
BLUEBERRY FLAN
ITALIAN CREAM COCONUT CAKE
FROZEN ENGLISH CUSTARD
BLACK FOREST CAKE

People probably serve and eat more desserts during the Christmas holidays than at any other time of year. Make yours sweetly memorable with the rich ingredients and appealing presentations of these recipes. Classic desserts can be an impressive finale to a holiday dinner or the center of attraction for a Christmas coffee.

RASPBERRY TART
Easy Puff Pastry (recipe follows)
1 egg, beaten
1 teaspoon water
2 (10-ounce) packages frozen raspberries
  in syrup, thawed
1½ tablespoons cornstarch
¼ cup sugar
3 egg yolks, beaten
¼ cup half-and-half
3 tablespoons brandy
1 teaspoon almond extract
Sugar-frosted grapes (recipe follows)

Roll pastry on a well-floured surface to a 16½ x 9-inch rectangle; refrigerate 15 to 20 minutes. Cut a ¾-inch strip from each side of pastry. Place rectangle on an ungreased baking sheet, and brush edges lightly with cold water. Place strips on edges of rectangle, trimming ends. Seal strips to pastry around edges with tines of a fork. Combine egg and 1 teaspoon water; mix well, and brush on pastry strips. Pierce bottom of pastry rectangle all over with fork; refrigerate

15 minutes. Bake at 425° for 10 to 15 minutes or until golden. Cool.

Press raspberries through a sieve; reserve juice. Bring juice to a boil in a heavy saucepan; boil until reduced to ⅔ cup (about 5 minutes). Cool.

Combine cornstarch and sugar in a small saucepan. Combine raspberry juice, egg yolks, and half-and-half, beating well; add to cornstarch mixture, stirring until smooth. Cook over medium heat, stirring constantly, until thickened. Remove from heat; cool slightly, and stir in brandy and almond extract. Cover and cool to room temperature.

Spread cooled custard on pastry. Arrange sugar-frosted grapes attractively on tart. Yield: one 15 x 7½-inch tart.

Easy Puff Pastry:
2½ cups all-purpose flour
½ teaspoon salt
¾ pound butter, frozen and cut into
  pieces
⅓ cup plain yogurt
1 egg, beaten

Position knife blade in processor bowl. Add flour and salt, and process to combine, pulsing 2 or 3 times. Distribute frozen butter evenly over flour mixture; process just until mixture forms coarse crumbs. Add yogurt and egg; process just until dough almost forms a ball. (Do not over-process dough; lumps of butter should be visible.)

Pat dough into a rectangle on a generously floured surface; roll into a 24 x 8-inch rectangle (dough will be about ¼-inch thick). Fold short ends in to meet at the center; fold in half like a book. Wrap dough with plastic wrap, and refrigerate 20 minutes. Turn dough so that folded edge is facing you; repeat rolling and folding instructions, working quickly so butter does not soften. Wrap in

---

For unforgettably delicious desserts, try the deluxe recipes and elegant presentations offered here. Clockwise from right: Raspberry Tart, Frozen English Custard, and Chocolate Orange Meringue Torte.

plastic wrap; refrigerate 4 hours or overnight before shaping. Yield: enough pastry for a 15 x 7½-inch tart.

Note: Easy Puff Pastry may be frozen up to 6 months. Thaw in refrigerator before using.

Sugar-Frosted Grapes:
1 pound green grapes, separated into clusters
½ cup lemon juice
About 1 cup sugar

Dip clusters of grapes into lemon juice. Sprinkle grapes lightly with sugar; repeat sprinkling to build more layers of sugar. Place on a wire rack, and refrigerate until coating is set. Yield: 1 pound.

LIME CREAM DESSERT
1 envelope unflavored gelatin
¼ cup cold water
½ cup lime juice
¼ cup plus 2 tablespoons orange juice
½ cup sugar
½ teaspoon grated lime rind
1 egg white
¼ teaspoon salt
3 tablespoons sugar
1 cup whipping cream, whipped
Fresh lime slices (optional)
Whipped cream (optional)
Grated lime rind (optional)

Dissolve gelatin in cold water; set aside.

Combine lime juice, orange juice, ½ cup sugar, and ½ teaspoon lime rind in a small saucepan; bring to a boil, stirring frequently. Stir gelatin into juice mixture. Chill until the consistency of unbeaten egg white.

Beat egg white (at room temperature) and salt until foamy. Gradually add 3 tablespoons sugar, beating until stiff peaks form.

Fold egg white and whipped cream into juice mixture. Pour into an oiled 1-quart mold; chill until set. To serve, unmold and garnish with lime slices. Top with a dollop of whipped cream and grated lime rind, if desired. Yield: 6 to 8 servings.

CHOCOLATE ORANGE MERINGUE TORTE
6 egg whites
½ teaspoon cream of tartar
¼ teaspoon salt
1 teaspoon vanilla extract
1 cup superfine sugar
1 (12-ounce) package semisweet chocolate morsels, divided
1 tablespoon shortening
¼ cup orange marmalade
2 cups whipping cream
⅔ cup sifted powdered sugar
2 teaspoons grated orange rind
Candied orange slices (optional)
Chocolate curls (optional)

Line 2 baking sheets with aluminum foil; grease foil lightly, and dust with flour. Draw 2 (8-inch) circles on 1 baking sheet, and 1 (8-inch) circle on the other; set aside.

Beat egg whites (at room temperature) in a large mixing bowl at high speed of an electric mixer until foamy; sprinkle cream of tartar, salt, and vanilla over egg whites, and continue beating until soft peaks form. Gradually add superfine sugar, 1 tablespoon at a time, beating until stiff peaks form. Spread meringue inside ring outlines to edges, smoothing tops with a spatula. Bake at 250° for 2 hours or until light golden in color, reversing oven racks after 1 hour. Turn off oven; cool in oven 6 hours or overnight. Carefully loosen layers from foil.

Melt 1½ cups chocolate morsels and 1 tablespoon shortening in top of a double boiler over hot water; cool slightly. Drizzle evenly over meringue layers, and spread chocolate in a thin layer to cover tops and sides of layers. Refrigerate 20 minutes or until chocolate hardens.

Melt remaining ½ cup chocolate morsels in top of a double boiler. Remove chocolate from hot water, and stir in marmalade. Cool completely. Beat whipping cream in a large bowl until foamy; gradually add powdered sugar and orange rind, beating until stiff peaks form. Measure and reserve 1½ cups whipped cream for piping. Stir ¼ cup of remaining whipped cream into chocolate mixture; fold in remaining whipped cream.

Stack 2 meringue layers on a serving plate, dividing and spreading the chocolate whipped cream mixture evenly on top of the two layers. Top with remaining meringue layer; spread or pipe reserved plain whipped cream mixture on top, using No. 5 or 6B large fluted tip. Garnish with candied orange slices and chocolate curls if desired. Refrigerate at least 1 hour but not more than 4 hours. Yield: one 8-inch torte.

WHITE APRICOT-GLAZED FRUITCAKE
3 cups (about 1 pound) dried figs, diced
2¼ cups golden raisins
2 cups diced dried apricots
⅓ cup rum or brandy
2 tablespoons shortening, melted
2½ cups sifted cake flour
2 teaspoons baking powder
1 teaspoon salt
2 cups diced candied pineapple
2 cups coarsely chopped walnuts
1½ cups coarsely chopped almonds
1 cup butter or margarine
1½ cups sugar
7 eggs, separated
1 cup milk
1 tablespoon vanilla extract
1½ cups flaked coconut
Rum
Apricot Glaze
Additional dried fruit and nuts for garnish

Combine figs, raisins, apricots, and rum in a large bowl. Cover with plastic wrap; let stand at room temperature overnight, stirring mixture occasionally.

Lightly brush a 10-inch tube pan with half of melted shortening; line pan with parchment or brown paper. (Do not use recycled paper.) Brush paper with remaining melted shortening; set pan aside.

Combine flour, baking powder, and salt in a large bowl, stirring well. Add candied pineapple, walnuts, and almonds to fig mixture, mixing well. Sprinkle ¼ cup flour mixture over fruit mixture. Toss well, coating fruit and nuts thoroughly. Reserve remaining flour mixture.

Cream butter in a large mixing bowl; gradually add sugar, beating at medium speed of an electric mixer until light and fluffy. Add egg yolks, 1 at a time, beating well after each addition. Combine milk and vanilla. Add remaining flour mixture to creamed mixture alternately with milk mixture, beginning and ending with dry ingredients. (Batter will be stiff.) Stir in reserved fruit mixture and coconut, mixing well.

Beat egg whites (at room temperature) in a large mixing bowl until stiff peaks form. Stir ¼ cup beaten egg whites into cake batter; carefully fold in remaining egg whites. Pour batter into prepared pan. Tap gently on countertop to level batter; smooth top with spatula. Place in lower third of oven; bake at 275° for 2 hours to 2 hours and 20 minutes or until a long, wooden pick inserted in center comes out clean, but slightly sticky.

Cool cake in pan on a wire rack 15 minutes; remove from pan, and remove paper. Cool upright on a wire rack. When completely cooled, wrap in a rum-soaked cheesecloth, and store in an airtight container in refrigerator for at least 2 weeks.

Remove cake from refrigerator 1 to 2 hours before glazing. Brush a thin layer of Apricot Glaze over top and sides of cake; decorate with additional fruit and nuts as desired. Let stand 10 minutes; brush with another thin layer of glaze. Store in refrigerator. Yield: one 10-inch cake.

Apricot Glaze:

1 (10-ounce) jar apricot preserves
2 teaspoons lemon juice

Cook preserves in a small saucepan over low heat, stirring constantly, until melted; simmer 2 minutes. Remove from heat, and strain to remove pulp; stir in lemon juice. Use immediately to glaze cake. Yield: ½ cup.

BLUEBERRY FLAN

⅓ cup butter or margarine, softened
⅔ cup sugar
3 egg yolks
⅓ cup milk
1 cup all-purpose flour
1 teaspoon cream of tartar
½ teaspoon baking soda
¼ teaspoon salt
½ teaspoon almond extract
Blueberry Filling
Whipped cream

Combine butter and sugar; cream until light and fluffy. Add egg yolks and milk, beating well. Combine dry ingredients; add to butter mixture, and beat well. Stir in almond extract.

Pour batter into a greased and floured 10-inch flan pan. Bake at 350° for 20 minutes. Remove from pan; cool. Spoon Blueberry Filling into center of flan. Serve with whipped cream. Yield: about 8 servings.

Blueberry Filling:

¼ cup all-purpose flour
1 cup sugar
⅛ teaspoon salt
¼ teaspoon almond extract
3 cups fresh or frozen blueberries
1 tablespoon butter or margarine

Combine flour, sugar, salt, and almond extract in a saucepan; gently stir in berries. Add butter; cook over low heat, stirring occasionally, until thickened. Cool. Yield: 3¼ cups.

ITALIAN CREAM COCONUT CAKE

1 cup butter or margarine, softened
2 cups sugar
5 eggs, separated
2 teaspoons vanilla extract
2 cups all-purpose flour
1 teaspoon baking soda
1 cup buttermilk
2 cups flaked coconut, divided
1 cup chopped walnuts, divided
Cream Cheese Frosting
Red and green candied cherries

Cream butter; gradually add sugar, beating until light and fluffy. Add egg yolks, one at a time, beating well after each addition. Stir in vanilla.

Combine flour and soda; add to creamed mixture alternately with buttermilk, beginning and ending with flour mixture. Stir in 1 cup coconut and ½ cup walnuts.

Beat egg whites (at room temperature) until stiff peaks form; fold into batter. Pour mixture into 3 greased and floured 8-inch cakepans. Bake at 350° for 25 to 30 minutes or until a wooden pick inserted in center comes out clean.

Cool in pans 10 minutes; turn out onto wire racks, and cool completely.

Spread Cream Cheese Frosting between layers; sprinkle each layer with ⅓ cup coconut and ¼ cup walnuts. Spread remaining frosting on top and sides of cake, and sprinkle top with remaining ⅓ cup coconut. Garnish with candied cherries as desired. Yield: one 3-layer cake.

Cream Cheese Frosting:

½ cup butter or margarine, softened
1 (8-ounce) package cream cheese, softened
1 (16-ounce) package powdered sugar
2 teaspoons vanilla extract

Combine butter and cream cheese, beating until light and fluffy. Add powdered sugar and vanilla; beat until smooth. Yield: enough for one 8-inch 3-layer cake.

custard using No. 5 or 6B large fluted tip; decorate with additional pistachio nuts and candied cherries as desired. Cut into wedges to serve. Yield: 8 to 10 servings.

FROZEN ENGLISH CUSTARD
½ cup golden raisins
⅓ cup currants
½ cup brandy
1¾ cups fine shortbread cookie crumbs
¼ cup plus 2 tablespoons butter or margarine, melted
2 (3-ounce) packages vanilla pudding mix
3 cups milk
⅔ cup chopped candied cherries
⅔ cup chopped dry-roasted pistachio nuts
1 teaspoon vanilla extract
2 cups whipping cream, whipped and divided
Additional chopped dry-roasted pistachio nuts
Additional candied cherries

Combine raisins, currants, and brandy in a small bowl; cover with plastic wrap, and let stand at room temperature overnight.

Line a 1½-quart bowl or tall mold with aluminum foil. Combine cookie crumbs and butter; press mixture firmly into foil-lined bowl to line it. Chill until firm.

Prepare pudding mix according to package directions, using 3 cups milk instead of 4 cups as package directs. Cool completely. Stir in raisin mixture, ⅔ cup candied cherries, ⅔ cup pistachio nuts, and vanilla, mixing well. Fold 3 cups whipped cream into pudding mixture. Pour into cookie-lined bowl; cover with plastic wrap, and freeze 8 hours or until firm.

To unmold, invert bowl onto a serving plate; carefully peel off foil. Pipe remaining whipped cream around bottom of frozen

BLACK FOREST CAKE
2¼ cups all-purpose flour
2 cups sugar
½ cup plus 2 tablespoons cocoa
1½ teaspoons baking powder
¾ teaspoon baking soda
¾ teaspoon salt
½ cup shortening
3 eggs
1 cup milk
1 tablespoon vanilla extract
3 cups whipping cream
¼ cup plus 2 tablespoons powdered sugar
1 (21-ounce) can cherry pie filling

Combine first 6 ingredients in a large mixing bowl; stir until well mixed. Add shortening, eggs, milk, and vanilla; beat mixture 3 minutes at low speed of an electric mixer, scraping bowl occasionally.

Grease two 9-inch cakepans; line bottom with waxed paper. Pour batter into pans. Bake at 350° for 30 to 35 minutes or until a wooden pick inserted in center comes out clean. Cool cake in pans 10 minutes; remove from pans, and cool completely.

Split cake layers in half horizontally to make 4 layers. Make fine crumbs using 1 cake layer; set crumbs aside.

Beat whipping cream until foamy; gradually add powdered sugar, beating until soft peaks form. Place 1 cake layer on cake platter; spread with 1 cup whipped cream, and top with ¾ cup cherry pie filling. Repeat with second layer; then top with third cake layer. Frost sides and top with whipped cream, reserving a small amount for garnish. Pat cake crumbs generously around sides of cake. (There may be leftover cake crumbs.) Spoon dollops of whipped cream around top of cake; spoon remaining pie filling on top of cake. Chill well. Yield: one 9-inch cake.

MAKE IT QUICK WITH A MICROWAVE

> *TOMATO CREAM SOUP*
> *CHICKEN SALAD PINWHEELS*
> *TURKEY REUBEN CASSEROLE*
> *RICE AND HAM RAVIGOTE*
> *PORK AND PINEAPPLE PIE*
> *CRAB AND MUSHROOM AU GRATIN*
> *NUTTY CARAMEL CHEWS*

In the midst of all the exciting things to do during the holidays, there may be times when you need to prepare good food very quickly. With a microwave oven and these carefully tested recipes, you can save time without skimping on flavor or nutrition.

TOMATO CREAM SOUP

1 cup water
1 (28-ounce) can whole tomatoes, undrained and coarsely chopped
1 medium onion, coarsely chopped
1 medium baking potato, peeled and cut into 1-inch cubes
3 bay leaves
½ teaspoon dried whole basil
2 (10¾-ounce) cans chicken broth, undiluted
½ cup whipping cream
¼ teaspoon white pepper
Minced fresh parsley (optional)

Combine first 6 ingredients in a 2½-quart microwave-safe casserole; cover with heavy-duty plastic wrap. Microwave at HIGH for 18 minutes or until vegetables are tender, stirring every 5 minutes. Remove bay leaves.

With these delicious dishes, no one will ever know you didn't have all day to prepare for dinner. Back to front: Pork and Pineapple Pie, Rice and Ham Ravigote, and Tomato Cream Soup.

Transfer half of mixture to container of an electric blender; process until smooth. Strain mixture through a fine-meshed sieve into a large bowl. Repeat process, using remaining vegetable mixture.

Add chicken broth, cream, and white pepper to bowl; stir well. Cover and microwave at HIGH for 7 to 8 minutes or until thoroughly heated (do not boil). Serve in bowls; sprinkle with parsley, if desired. Yield: 7¾ cups.

CHICKEN SALAD PINWHEELS

1 (5-ounce) can chunk chicken, drained and flaked
¼ cup sliced water chestnuts, minced
¼ cup mayonnaise
2 tablespoons minced green onion
1 tablespoon diced pimiento
1 teaspoon lemon juice
12 slices whole wheat sandwich bread
¼ cup butter or margarine
1 egg, beaten
½ cup sesame seeds, toasted

Combine first 6 ingredients; mix well, and set aside. Trim crusts from bread; roll bread to ¼-inch thickness using a rolling pin. Spread chicken mixture on bread slices; roll up jellyroll fashion.

Place butter in a pieplate; microwave at HIGH for 55 seconds or until melted. Beat egg into butter. Roll sandwich rolls in butter mixture; then roll in sesame seeds, coating well. Place on a baking sheet, and freeze 30 minutes or until firm; wrap rolls in aluminum foil, and freeze up to 2 weeks.

To serve, cut each frozen roll into 4 pieces. Place one-half of pieces around edge of a paper towel-lined (double thickness) 12-inch round glass plate. Cover with a paper towel; microwave at MEDIUM HIGH (80% power) for 3 minutes or until hot, rotating plate at 1-minute intervals. Repeat with remaining pieces. Yield: 4 dozen.

TURKEY REUBEN CASSEROLE

⅓ cup butter or margarine
1 cup whole grain rye cracker crumbs
¼ teaspoon caraway seeds
1 (16-ounce) can sauerkraut, well drained
1 medium-size green pepper, chopped
¾ cup commercial Thousand Island
   dressing, divided
2 cups shredded, cooked turkey
2 cups (8 ounces) shredded Swiss cheese
1 large tomato, peeled and sliced

Place the butter in a 4-cup glass measure. Microwave at HIGH for 1 minute or until melted. Add whole grain rye cracker crumbs and caraway seeds; then mix well, and set aside.

Spread sauerkraut evenly in a lightly greased 2-quart microwave-safe casserole; sprinkle with green pepper. Spoon half of dressing evenly over green pepper; top with turkey and remaining dressing. Cover with heavy-duty plastic wrap, and microwave at HIGH for 4 minutes. Layer cheese, tomato slices, and reserved cracker crumb mixture on top; microwave, uncovered, at HIGH for 3 to 4 minutes or until thoroughly heated. Let stand 2 minutes before serving. Yield: 6 servings.

RICE AND HAM RAVIGOTE

2 tablespoons butter or margarine
1 tablespoon plus 2 teaspoons all-purpose
   flour
½ cup orange juice
½ cup mayonnaise
½ teaspoon curry powder
¼ teaspoon red pepper
¼ teaspoon salt
3 cups cooked rice
3 cups (about 1 pound) diced ham
1 small green pepper, chopped
⅓ cup sliced green onion with tops
¼ cup sliced pimiento-stuffed olives
1 (11-ounce) can mandarin oranges,
   drained
¾ cup coarsely chopped peanuts

Place butter in a 2-quart microwave-safe casserole; microwave at HIGH for 45 seconds or until melted. Add flour, stirring until smooth. Gradually add orange juice, stirring well. Microwave at HIGH for 1½ minutes or until thickened and bubbly; stir well using a wire whisk. Add mayonnaise, curry powder, red pepper, and salt, mixing well; stir in next 5 ingredients. Cover with heavy-duty plastic wrap, and microwave at HIGH for 6 minutes. Gently stir in oranges; sprinkle peanuts around edge of dish. Microwave, uncovered, at HIGH for 2 minutes or until thoroughly heated. Yield: 6 servings.

PORK AND PINEAPPLE PIE

4 slices bacon
1 pound lean ground pork
½ pound bulk pork sausage
1 egg
2 tablespoons instant minced onion
1 teaspoon caraway seeds, crushed
½ teaspoon dried whole oregano,
   crushed
1 (15¼-ounce) can sliced pineapple
2 tablespoons butter or margarine
2 tablespoons all-purpose flour
⅓ cup half-and-half
¼ teaspoon salt
⅛ teaspoon white pepper
1 cup (4 ounces) shredded sharp Cheddar
   cheese

Arrange bacon in a 10-inch pieplate; cover with paper towels. Microwave at HIGH for 3½ to 4½ minutes or until bacon is crisp; drain bacon. Break 3 slices bacon in half crosswise; set aside. Roll up remaining slice bacon while warm to form a curl; set aside to cool. (Bacon curl will "set" as it cools.) Drain drippings from pieplate.

Combine next 6 ingredients; mix well. Press mixture into pieplate, shaping mixture up sides of pieplate to form a 1½-inch high rim. Cover with waxed paper; microwave at HIGH for 7 minutes or until firm to the touch, giving the dish a half-turn after 3 minutes. Drain off the excess drippings.

Drain pineapple, reserving juice. Place butter in a 4-cup glass measure; microwave at HIGH for 45 seconds or until melted. Add flour, stirring until smooth. Gradually add reserved pineapple juice and half-and-half, stirring well. Microwave at HIGH for 2 minutes; stir well. Microwave at HIGH for 2½ to 3½ minutes, stirring at 1-minute intervals until thickened and bubbly. Add salt, white pepper, and cheese; stir until cheese melts. Let stand 2 minutes.

Spoon cheese sauce into meat shell; arrange pineapple slices, overlapping, on sauce. Arrange bacon in a pinwheel over pineapple. Microwave at HIGH for 2 to 3 minutes or until thoroughly heated. Gently transfer to a serving platter using a wide spatula. Garnish center with reserved bacon curl. Yield: 6 to 8 servings.

CRAB AND MUSHROOM AU GRATIN
1 tablespoon butter or margarine
1 pound small fresh mushrooms
2 tablespoons butter or margarine
1 medium onion, chopped
1 tablespoon all-purpose flour
¾ cup mayonnaise or salad dressing
½ cup Chablis or other dry white wine
1 tablespoon lemon juice
2 (6½-ounce) cans crabmeat, drained and
    flaked
2 tablespoons butter or margarine
¾ cup fine, dry breadcrumbs
¾ cups (3 ounces) shredded mozzarella
    cheese
Toast points

Place 1 tablespoon butter in a shallow microwave-safe 1½-quart casserole. Microwave at HIGH for 35 seconds or until melted. Add mushrooms; cover with heavy-duty plastic wrap. Microwave at HIGH for 4 to 5 minutes or until tender, stirring after 2 minutes. Drain mushrooms; set aside.

Place 2 tablespoons butter in same casserole; microwave at HIGH for 45 seconds or

until melted. Add onion; cover and microwave at HIGH for 4 minutes or until tender. Add flour, stirring well; stir in mayonnaise, Chablis, and lemon juice. Microwave at HIGH for 3 to 4 minutes, stirring well at 1-minute intervals until smooth and thickened. Stir in crabmeat and reserved mushrooms. Cover and microwave at HIGH for 3 minutes; stir well.

Place 2 tablespoons butter in a 1-cup glass measure. Microwave at HIGH for 45 seconds or until melted. Combine melted butter and breadcrumbs; sprinkle over crabmeat mixture. Microwave, uncovered, at HIGH for 3 minutes or until thoroughly heated. Sprinkle with cheese; microwave, uncovered, at HIGH for 30 seconds or until cheese melts. Serve mixture over toast points. Yield: 6 to 8 servings.

NUTTY CARAMEL CHEWS
1 (14-ounce) package caramels
1½ tablespoons milk
1½ cups coarsely chopped walnuts
½ cup chopped candied cherries
1 (12-ounce) package semisweet chocolate
    morsels
1 tablespoon shortening

Remove any chocolate caramels in package, and reserve for another use. Unwrap remaining caramels, and place in a 2-quart casserole. Microwave at HIGH for 1 to 1¼ minutes; stir well.

Add milk to caramels, and microwave at HIGH for 1½ to 2 minutes, stirring every 30 seconds. Stir until mixture is smooth; add walnuts and cherries, mixing well. Drop by teaspoonfuls onto buttered waxed paper. Cool; cover and chill.

Combine chocolate morsels and shortening in a 4-cup glass measure. Microwave at MEDIUM (50% power) for 3 to 4 minutes or until morsels are softened; stir well. Dip caramel centers into chocolate, and return to waxed paper. Chill. Store candy in refrigerator. Yield: about 2½ dozen.

AN EVENING WITH THE FAMILY

ALMOND-TOPPED BRIE
PIMIENTO BROCCOLI
DUTCH MEAT LOAF
PARSLEYED FETTUCCINE
BREAKAWAY VEGETABLE BREAD
HOT BRANDIED FRUIT KABOBS
STRAWBERRY CREAM PUFFS OR
BROWNIE ALASKAS
This menu serves 6.

The Christmas feasts and festivities; the school, church, office, and club parties; the gift making, baking, buying, and wrapping; the visits with neighbors and friends—with all these activities, it's difficult to find time for a sit-down meal with just the family.

This easy-to-prepare meal is planned for an intimate family night—a quiet evening at home to catch up on everyone's busy schedule. It's a hearty, hot dinner to supply all that extra energy that the holidays demand.

ALMOND-TOPPED BRIE
1 (2½-pound) round fully ripened Brie
⅔ cup coarsely chopped almonds
2 to 3 tablespoons brown sugar

Remove rind from top of cheese, cutting to within ¼ inch of outside edges. Place cheese on an ungreased baking sheet, and arrange almonds over top. Sprinkle with sugar.

Broil 8 inches from heat for 3 to 5 minutes or until sugar and cheese are bubbly. Serve with crackers. Leftover cheese may be reheated, if desired. Yield: one cheese round.

Take time out with family to share holiday happenings over a delicious, easy-to-prepare meal. Front to back: Hot Brandied Fruit Kabobs, Pimiento Broccoli, and Dutch Meat Loaf over Parsleyed Fettuccine.

PIMIENTO BROCCOLI
¼ cup olive oil
1 teaspoon minced garlic
6 cups chopped fresh broccoli
1½ cups dry white wine
½ teaspoon salt
Freshly ground black pepper
2 tablespoons diced pimiento

Heat olive oil in heavy skillet; sauté garlic briefly. Add broccoli, stirring until coated. Stir in wine, salt, and pepper to taste; simmer, uncovered, 2 minutes, stirring occasionally. Cover and simmer 10 minutes.

Drain broccoli, reserving liquid; place broccoli in serving dish, and keep warm. Boil reserved liquid until reduced to ½ cup; stir in pimiento, and pour liquid over broccoli. Yield: 6 servings.

DUTCH MEAT LOAF
1½ pounds ground beef
1 cup soft breadcrumbs
1 small onion, finely chopped
⅓ cup finely chopped green pepper
2 eggs, beaten
1½ teaspoons salt
¼ teaspoon pepper
1 cup tomato sauce, divided
1 tablespoon brown sugar
1 tablespoon vinegar
1½ teaspoons prepared mustard
Chopped fresh parsley
Tomato rose (optional)

Combine beef, breadcrumbs, onion, green pepper, eggs, salt, pepper, and ½ cup tomato sauce; press into an 8½ x 4½ x 3-inch loafpan. Unmold loaf on rack of broiler pan. Bake at 350° for 1 hour.

Combine remaining 1/2 cup tomato sauce, brown sugar, vinegar, and mustard in a small saucepan; cook over medium heat until thoroughly heated.

Transfer loaf to platter. Spoon sauce over meat loaf. Sprinkle with parsley. Garnish platter with a tomato rose. Yield: 6 to 8 servings.

PARSLEYED FETTUCCINE

8 ounces fettuccine
¼ cup plus 2 tablespoons butter or
  margarine, melted
¼ cup grated Parmesan cheese
¼ cup chopped fresh parsley
Freshly ground pepper to taste

Cook fettuccine according to package directions; drain. Combine remaining ingredients, mixing well. Add fettuccine, and toss gently. Serve immediately. Yield: 6 servings.

BREAKAWAY VEGETABLE BREAD

1 (11-ounce) can refrigerated buttermilk
  biscuits
3 tablespoons butter or margarine, melted
3 slices bacon, cooked and crumbled
3 tablespoons grated Parmesan cheese
⅓ cup finely chopped onion
⅓ cup finely chopped green pepper

Cut biscuits into quarters; dip each piece in butter, and layer one-third in a lightly greased 6-cup Bundt pan. Sprinkle with half

of bacon, cheese, onion, and green pepper. Repeat layers until all ingredients are used, ending with biscuits. Bake at 350° for 25 minutes or until done. Yield: 6 to 8 servings.

HOT BRANDIED FRUIT KABOBS

2 (15¼-ounce) cans pineapple chunks
2 (17-ounce) cans apricot halves
2 (6-ounce) jars maraschino cherries
¼ cup butter or margarine
¼ cup plus 2 tablespoons firmly packed brown sugar
¼ cup brandy
¼ teaspoon ground cloves
¼ teaspoon ground cinnamon
Spinach leaves (optional)

Drain the fruit, and combine the juices; stir well, and set aside ¼ cup of the fruit juice mixture.

Melt butter; add sugar, stirring until smooth. Add ¼ cup reserved juice, brandy, and spices; stir until blended.

Alternate fruit on wooden skewers; place skewers in a shallow baking dish, and baste with juice mixture. Bake at 350° for 15 minutes, basting with juice mixture occasionally. Serve kabobs on a bed of spinach leaves, if desired. Yield: 6 to 8 servings.

STRAWBERRY CREAM PUFFS

1 cup water
½ cup butter or margarine
½ teaspoon salt
1 cup all-purpose flour
4 eggs
1 (10-ounce) package frozen strawberries, thawed
8 scoops (about 1 quart) strawberry ice cream
½ cup whipping cream, whipped
Powdered sugar

Bring water to a boil in a medium saucepan; add butter, and continue boiling until butter melts. Quickly add salt and flour all at once; beat with a wooden spoon until mix-

ture forms a ball that leaves the sides of the pan. Remove mixture from heat, and cool slightly.

Add eggs to flour mixture, one at a time, beating well after each addition. (Mixture will separate as each egg is added; continue beating until smooth and shiny.)

Pipe batter into 8 rosettes onto greased baking sheet using metal decorating tip No. 4B. Bake at 400° for 35 to 40 minutes or until golden brown and puffed. (Do not open oven during baking.) Cool thoroughly on a wire rack.

With a sharp knife, cut shells in half horizontally. Spoon strawberries into bottom halves of cream puffs. Top with a scoop of ice cream and a dollop of whipped cream; cover with top halves, and sprinkle lightly with powdered sugar. Serve immediately. Yield: 8 servings.

BROWNIE ALASKAS

1 (15.5-ounce) package fudge brownie mix
1½ pints strawberry ice cream
4 egg whites
Pinch of salt
½ cup sugar
Red and green cherry wedges

Prepare brownie mix according to package directions using a 9-inch square pan; let cool completely. Cut brownies into 3-inch squares. Arrange brownies on a cookie sheet; top each with a scoop of ice cream. Freeze at least 1 hour.

Beat egg whites (at room temperature) until foamy. Add salt, and gradually add sugar, 1 tablespoon at a time, beating until stiff peaks form.

Just before serving, remove ice cream-topped brownies from freezer. Quickly spread meringue over ice cream, sealing to edge of brownie. Bake at 500° for 2 to 3 minutes or until meringue is lightly browned. Garnish each with cherry wedges. Yield: 9 servings.

KIDS' PARTY

Have a party for the kids, featuring treats that they can help prepare. These snacks with personality are created from nutritional ingredients and are as much fun to make as they are to eat.

With just a little guidance, children can make the party favors. And small hands are the right size to decorate the cookies with candies and nuts.

VEGETABLE SANTA
1 medium cauliflower, separated into flowerets
2 medium carrots, pared and cut into ¼-inch slices
3 tablespoons water
1 cup cherry tomatoes, halved lengthwise
1 ripe olive, halved crosswise
1 (10-ounce) package frozen French-style green beans, thawed
¼ cup commercial Italian salad dressing
3 tablespoons butter or margarine, melted

Combine cauliflower, carrots, and water in a 2-quart casserole. Cover and microwave at HIGH for 3 to 4 minutes or until crisp-tender, stirring after 2 minutes. Let stand, covered, 3 minutes. Rinse under cold running water. Drain well.

Arrange carrots for face of Santa in a 5 x 3-inch rectangle in center of a large, round microwave-safe platter. Reserve 1 large caulifloweret; arrange remaining cauliflowerets, stem side down, on plate to form beard and hair, starting from long edges of rectangle. Arrange cherry tomatoes, cut sides down, in

a cone shape to form a hat; place reserved cauliflower at tip of hat. Place ripe olive halves on carrots for eyes, and arrange beans at top of beard for whiskers.

Combine dressing and butter; mix well, and pour evenly over vegetables. Cover with heavy-duty plastic wrap, and microwave at HIGH for 2 minutes or until thoroughly heated, rotating platter a half turn after 1 minute. Let stand, covered, 2 minutes. Yield: 8 to 10 servings.

CHRISTMAS TREE PIZZA WEDGES
2 tablespoons cornmeal
2 cups cooked rice
¼ cup biscuit mix
1 cup (4 ounces) shredded mozzarella cheese
1 egg, beaten
2 tablespoons water
1 (14-ounce) jar pizza sauce
1 (3½-ounce) package sliced pepperoni
1 large green pepper, cut into 16 thin strips
About 1½ cups popped corn
About ¼ cup sliced pimiento-stuffed olives
½ cup grated Parmesan cheese

Sprinkle a well-greased 12-inch pizza pan with cornmeal; set aside.

Combine rice, biscuit mix, and mozzarella cheese; toss well. Add egg and water; mix well. Press mixture into prepared pan. Spread pizza evenly over rice crust; arrange pepperoni over sauce.

Mark pizza into 8 wedges by placing green pepper strips side by side on top of pepperoni. (When pizza is cut into wedges, each wedge will be lined with green pepper strips.) Bake at 375° for 25 minutes. Arrange

When even the food is smiling at you, you can be sure it's going to be a fun party. Clockwise from bottom right: Vegetable Santa, Nutty Sesame Angels, Animal Ornaments, and Rudolph, the Reindeer Orange, with company.

popcorn in diagonal rows on each wedge to resemble a tree with popcorn strings; arrange olive slices on wedges for "ornaments." Sprinkle with Parmesan cheese; bake an additional 5 minutes. Cut into wedges, using pepper strips as guides. Yield: 8 servings.

NUTTY SESAME ANGELS
1 (10-ounce) package refrigerator buttermilk biscuits
1 egg, beaten
1 tablespoon water
About ½ cup sesame seeds
About ⅓ cup sliced almonds
About ⅓ cup slivered almonds
Maraschino cherries
Currants

Separate biscuits, and place close together on waxed paper. Roll dough to about ⅛-inch thickness; cut with a 4-inch angel cookie cutter. Invert angels on a lightly greased baking sheet. Combine egg and water; carefully brush on angels. Sprinkle sesame seeds on angel wings, and place almonds on angel dresses and as headpieces. Place a small piece of cherry on each angel for mouth, and currants for eyes and noses. Bake at 400° for 8 minutes or until golden brown. Remove from oven. Carefully slip a spatula under angels to loosen; let cool 1 minute on baking sheet. Transfer to wire rack to cool completely. Yield: 8 to 10 angels.

STRAWBERRY PEPPERMINT SLUSH
2 (10-ounce) packages frozen strawberries in light syrup
2 cups milk, divided
6 (8-ounce) cartons strawberry yogurt, frozen
½ teaspoon peppermint extract, divided
8 peppermint candy canes (optional)

Combine 1 package strawberries and 1 cup milk in container of an electric blender; process at medium speed until smooth. Add 3 cartons yogurt; process at low speed until

thick and smooth. Add ¼ teaspoon peppermint extract; process until blended. Pour into glasses; place a candy cane in each glass, if desired, and serve immediately. Repeat procedure with remaining ingredients. Yield: 8 cups.

ANIMAL ORNAMENTS
½ cup shortening
¾ cup sugar
1 egg
½ teaspoon vanilla extract
1 tablespoon grated orange rind
1 tablespoon grated lemon rind
¼ cup orange juice
2½ cups all-purpose flour
¼ teaspoon salt
½ teaspoon baking powder
½ teaspoon baking soda
1 egg yolk
¼ teaspoon water
Liquid food coloring
Assorted candies and nuts

Cream shortening; gradually add sugar, beating until light and fluffy. Stir in egg, vanilla, citrus rind, and juice, mixing well. Combine dry ingredients; add to creamed

mixture, mixing well (mixture will be very stiff). Divide dough in half; gather each half into a ball. Wrap and chill thoroughly.

Roll each portion of dough to ⅛-inch thickness on a lightly floured surface. Cut with 2½-inch animal-shaped cookie cutters, and transfer to lightly greased cookie sheets. Punch a hole in top of each cookie with a clean drinking straw. (This will enable you to tie a ribbon through the cookie to hang on a tree.)

Combine egg yolk and water; mix well, and divide among 4 small bowls. Add 2 to 3 drops of a different food coloring to each bowl; mix well. Paint cookies as desired, using a clean small paint brush. (Dip brush in water when changing colors. If yolk mixture thickens while standing, stir in additional water, a drop at a time.) Finish decorating cookie with assorted candies and nuts. Bake at 300° for 12 to 14 minutes. Cool completely on wire racks. Tie cookie to Christmas tree with ribbon. Yield: 3½ dozen.

RUDOLPH, THE REINDEER ORANGE
8 medium oranges

Draw a reindeer face on each orange (or have children do it themselves) with black and red permanent ink markers. Draw and cut out paper antlers for each orange using brown construction paper. To attach, cut slits in top of each orange the width of the bottom of antlers; slip antlers into oranges.

To make oranges stand up, cut eight 4 x 1-inch strips of cardboard. Overlap ends of each strip, and staple together. Place decorated orange on holder. Yield: 8 servings.

CELEBRATE NEW YEAR'S EVE

HOT SPINACH BACON DIP
HOLIDAY BEEF BRISKET
APRICOT CHICKEN
TOMATO LEEK TART
THE KING'S BUTTER CAKE
BRANDIED FRUIT COMPOTE
COFFEE ELEGANTÉ
SWEDISH GLOGG

Celebrate the end of the old year and toast the new one with good friends and good food. Set the scene for a joyous celebration with this buffet dinner that features a diverse selection of taste sensations. It is a meal of party foods for a munching and mingling crowd. These dishes should satisfy the nibblers as well as the hungriest guests. Include a few recipes with a new twist, like the Tomato Leek Tart, for those ready to start the year off with something new.

HOT SPINACH BACON DIP
1 (10-ounce) package frozen chopped
    spinach
10 slices bacon
½ cup finely chopped onion
1 (8-ounce) package cream cheese
½ cup mayonnaise
¼ cup milk
¼ teaspoon hot sauce
½ cup chopped pecans

Start an evening of good cheer with a buffet dinner. Serve a variety of dishes, old favorites as well as new and unusual tempters. On the table, clockwise from bottom: Tomato Leek Tart, Holiday Beef Brisket, and Hot Spinach Bacon Dip. On the sideboard, left to right: Coffee Eleganté, Brandied Fruit Compote, and The King's Butter Cake.

Cook spinach according to package directions; drain well, and set aside.

Cook bacon in a large skillet until crisp; remove bacon, reserving 2 tablespoons drippings in skillet. Crumble bacon, and set aside. Sauté onion in drippings until tender. Add spinach and next 4 ingredients to skillet; mix well. Cook over low heat, stirring constantly, until cheese melts and mixture is thoroughly blended. Stir in crumbled bacon. Transfer to a heatproof serving dish or fondue pot; sprinkle with pecans. Serve hot with breadsticks or crackers. Yield: 3 cups.

HOLIDAY BEEF BRISKET
¼ cup whole juniper berries
1½ tablespoons whole allspice
1½ tablespoons whole peppercorns
1 teaspoon salt
1 teaspoon ground cinnamon
¼ cup firmly packed brown sugar
1 (4-pound) boneless beef brisket
1 cup water

Combine first 5 ingredients in container of an electric blender; process until ground to powder, scraping blender occasionally. Combine spice and sugar mixture, mixing well. Place beef in a 13 x 9 x 2-inch baking pan; rub spice mixture over meat, covering meat completely. Pour water into pan. Weight down beef evenly with a heavy object (bricks wrapped in foil or an oven bag work well); cover baking pan tightly with aluminum foil, and bake at 275° for 3½ hours. Remove from oven, and cool. Remove weight; scrape spices from meat. Wipe meat with a damp cloth to remove any spice mixture clinging to meat; wrap meat in foil. Place in a clean baking pan, and weight meat as directed above. Refrigerate at least 24 hours before serving. Slice thinly, and serve cold with commercial spicy mustard and assorted fresh breads. Yield: 20 appetizer servings.

Note: Do not use juniper berries that have been sprayed with insecticide or other harmful substances.

APRICOT CHICKEN

8 boneless chicken breast halves
1 (6-ounce) package dried apricots
1 (8-ounce) can whole water chestnuts, drained
½ cup soy sauce
½ cup dry sherry
¼ cup honey
2 tablespoons lemon juice
½ teaspoon ground ginger

Flatten each chicken breast half to ½-inch thickness, using a meat mallet or rolling pin. Cut into 1-inch-wide strips. Place chicken strips, apricots, and water chestnuts in a shallow container. Combine remaining ingredients; pour over chicken mixture, and mix well. Cover and refrigerate overnight, stirring occasionally.

Remove chicken, apricots, and water chestnuts from marinade; thread on 20 (6-inch) wooden skewers. Cover ends of skewers with aluminum foil. Place skewers on rack in a broiler pan; broil 6 inches from heat source 10 to 12 minutes, turning skewers and basting with marinade every 3 minutes. Serve hot or at room temperature. Yield: 20 appetizer servings.

TOMATO LEEK TART

1 (17½-ounce) package frozen puff pastry
1½ cups thinly sliced leeks
3 tablespoons butter or margarine, melted
1 (8-ounce) package cream cheese, cubed and softened
4 ounces blue cheese, crumbled
2 tablespoons milk
2 cloves garlic, crushed
3 tablespoons olive oil
1 (28-ounce) can whole tomatoes, drained and finely chopped
1 teaspoon dried whole basil
½ teaspoon freshly ground pepper
¼ teaspoon dried whole thyme
Leek tops

Lightly grease and flour a large baking sheet. Place pastry rectangles on baking sheet, and thaw at room temperature 20 minutes.

Unfold both rectangles of pastry. Roll pastry into two 10 x 8-inch rectangles; cut a ¾-inch-wide strip from each side of 1 rectangle, using a sharp knife. Brush edges of other pastry rectangle with water. Place the 4 pastry strips on top of sides of large pastry rectangle; trim ends so strips don't overlap. Reserve unused portion of pastry for other uses. Prick bottom of pastry all over with tines of a fork. Bake at 375° for 25 to 30 minutes or until puffed and golden brown. Cool completely on a wire rack.

Sauté sliced leeks in butter in a large skillet 5 minutes. Stir in cream cheese, blue cheese, and milk; cook over low heat, stirring constantly, until cheese melts. Cool to room temperature.

Sauté garlic in olive oil 1 minute in a large skillet. Add next 4 ingredients; simmer 10 minutes or until liquid has evaporated, stirring occasionally. Cool mixture to room temperature.

Blanch leek tops in boiling water 1 minute. Rinse under cold running water; drain and pat dry. Cut tops lengthwise into long, narrow strips, and set aside.

To assemble, spread cheese mixture evenly over pastry; spread tomato mixture on top. Arrange leek strips over tomato mixture, lattice fashion. Serve cold or at room temperature. Yield: 20 appetizer servings.

THE KING'S BUTTER CAKE

3 cups plus 2 tablespoons all-purpose flour
1¼ cups sugar
1 tablespoon grated lemon rind
¼ teaspoon ground mace
6 egg yolks, beaten
1 cup plus 2 tablespoons butter, cut into small pieces
1 egg yolk
1 tablespoon water

Butter a 9-inch springform pan, and line bottom with waxed paper; set aside.

Combine flour, sugar, lemon rind, and

mace in a large bowl. Make a well in center of mixture, and add beaten egg yolks; stir until mixture resembles coarse meal. Sprinkle butter pieces evenly over mixture; knead until butter is incorporated and dough is blended. Press dough evenly into pan.

Combine 1 egg yolk and water; beat well. Brush dough with egg wash. Score top of dough with tines of a fork to form diamond or flower pattern. Bake at 350° for 1 hour or until surface of cake is dark golden brown and feels firm when touched in center.

Remove cake from oven, and immediately rub top very lightly with a clean kitchen towel to make surface of cake shine. Remove side of pan; cool 15 minutes on a wire rack. Remove bottom of pan, and peel away waxed paper; cool completely on a wire rack. Slice into thin wedges. Yield: one 1-layer cake.

BRANDIED FRUIT COMPOTE

4 cups seedless green grapes, halved
5 medium oranges, peeled, seeded, and
    sectioned
1 (15¼-ounce) can pineapple chunks,
    drained
½ cup brandy
3 tablespoons minced crystallized ginger
1 (16-ounce) can pitted dark sweet
    cherries, drained
¾ cup chopped walnuts

Combine first 5 ingredients in a large bowl; toss well. Cover and refrigerate at least 4 hours or until serving time, stirring occasionally. Stir in cherries and walnuts just before serving. Yield: 8 cups or 20 appetizer servings.

COFFEE ELEGANTÉ

8 cups water
1½ teaspoons whole allspice
3 (3-inch) sticks cinnamon
2 whole vanilla beans
8 tablespoons medium-grind coffee
Cinnamon-Chocolate Whipped Cream

Combine first 4 ingredients in a medium saucepan; bring to a boil. Reduce heat and simmer, uncovered, 10 minutes. Remove from heat, and cool.

Assemble drip coffeemaker according to manufacturer's instructions. Place ground coffee in paper filter or filter basket; pour spiced water into coffeemaker, and brew. Serve immediately with Cinnamon-Chocolate Whipped Cream. Yield: 10 cups.

Cinnamon-Chocolate Whipped Cream:

1 tablespoon plus 2 teaspoons sweetened
    cocoa mix
2 tablespoons powdered sugar
¼ teaspoon ground cinnamon
1 cup whipping cream
¼ teaspoon vanilla extract

Combine first 3 ingredients, mixing well. Beat whipping cream and vanilla at high speed of an electric mixer until foamy; gradually add cocoa mixture, beating until stiff peaks form. Serve with coffee. Yield: 2 cups.

SWEDISH GLOGG

3⅓ cups red Bordeaux wine
3⅓ cups port wine
2 medium oranges, sliced
20 whole cloves
12 cardamom seeds
2 (3-inch) sticks cinnamon
¾ cup superfine sugar
1 cup whole almonds
1 cup raisins
3 cups brandy

Combine first 7 ingredients in a large saucepan; cook over low heat, stirring constantly, until sugar dissolves. Bring almost to a boil; cover, remove from heat, and let stand 10 minutes.

Place almonds and raisins in a heatproof punch bowl. Heat brandy (do not boil). Strain hot wine into punch bowl; stir in brandy. Ladle into punch cups, placing a few almonds and raisins in each cup. Yield: 10 cups.

PATTERNS
TWINKLING HEARTS IN PUNCHED TIN
instructions on page 2
full-size patterns

Repeat and adapt patterns as necessary to fit your containers.

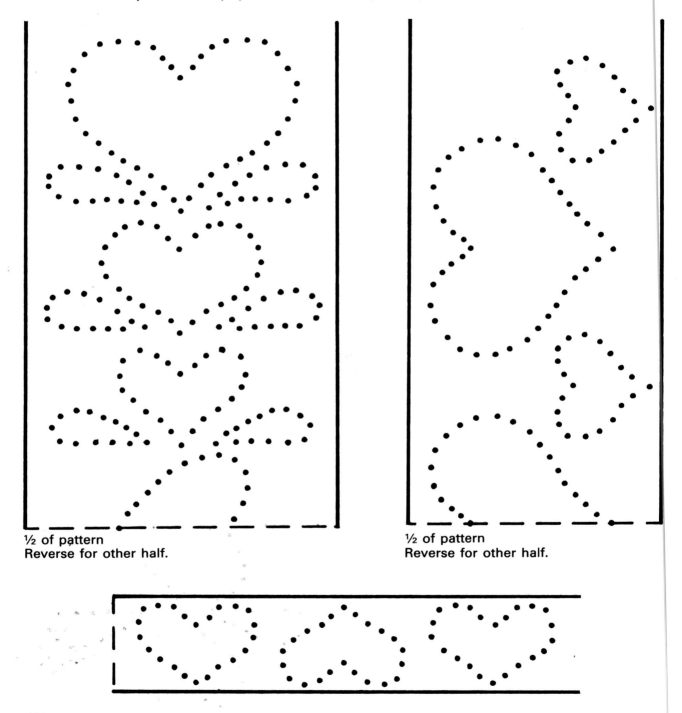

½ of pattern
Reverse for other half.

½ of pattern
Reverse for other half.

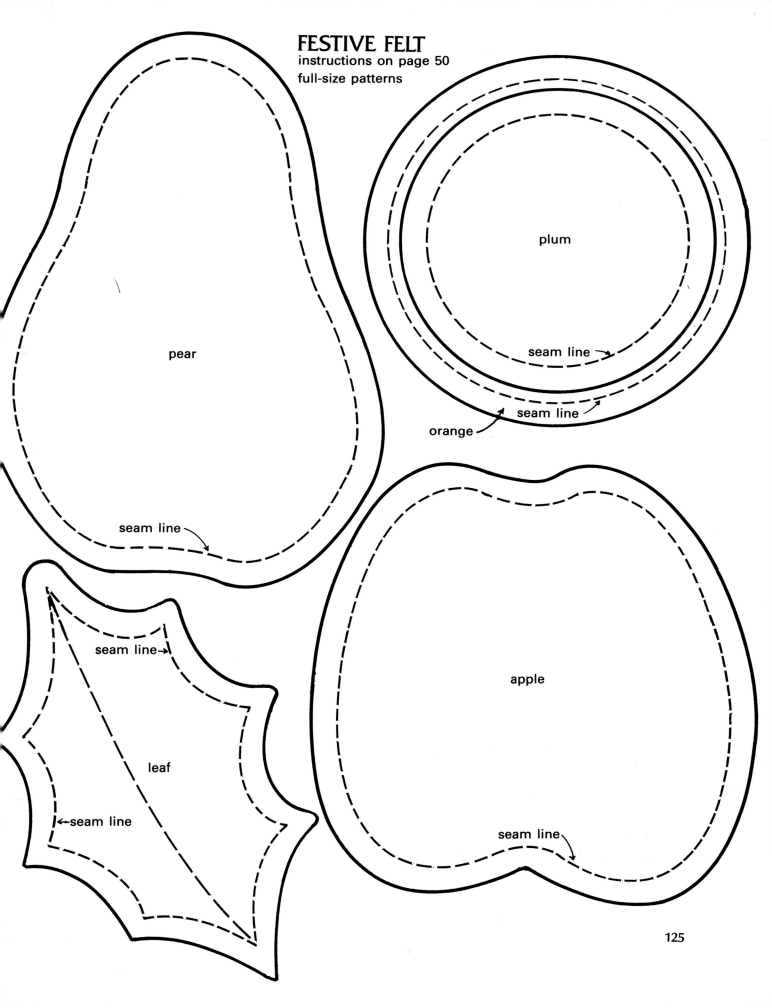

FESTIVE FELT
instructions on page 50
full-size patterns

pear

seam line

plum

seam line →

seam line →

orange

apple

seam line

seam line→

leaf

←seam line

seam line

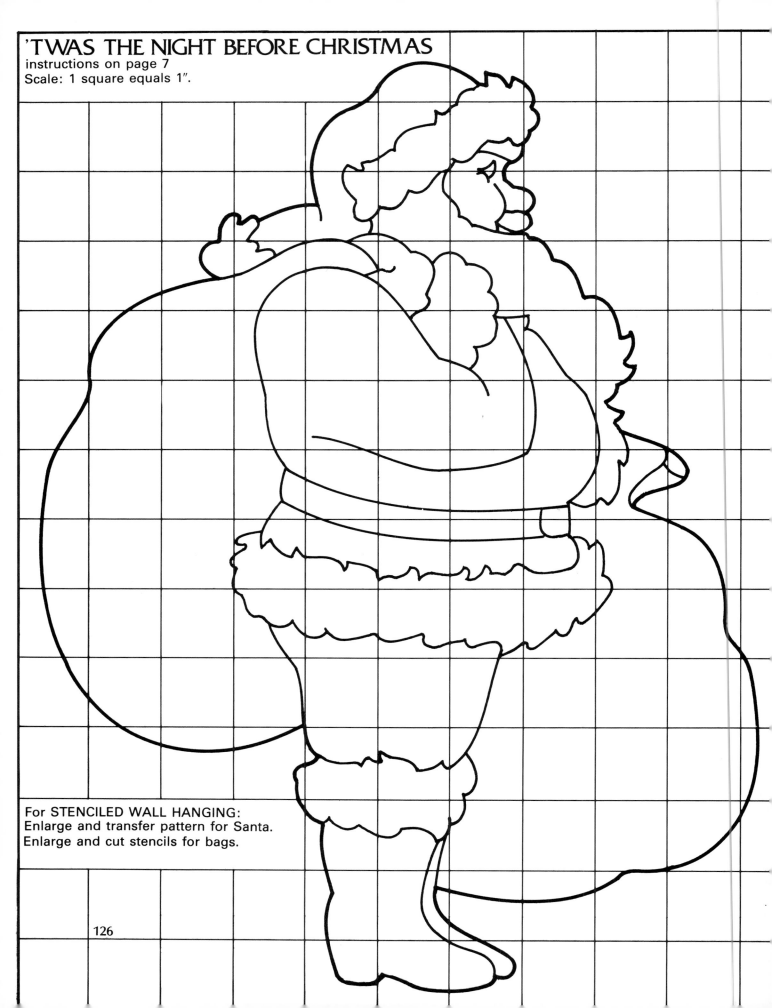

'TWAS THE NIGHT BEFORE CHRISTMAS
instructions on page 7
Scale: 1 square equals 1″.

For STENCILED WALL HANGING:
Enlarge and transfer pattern for Santa.
Enlarge and cut stencils for bags.

126

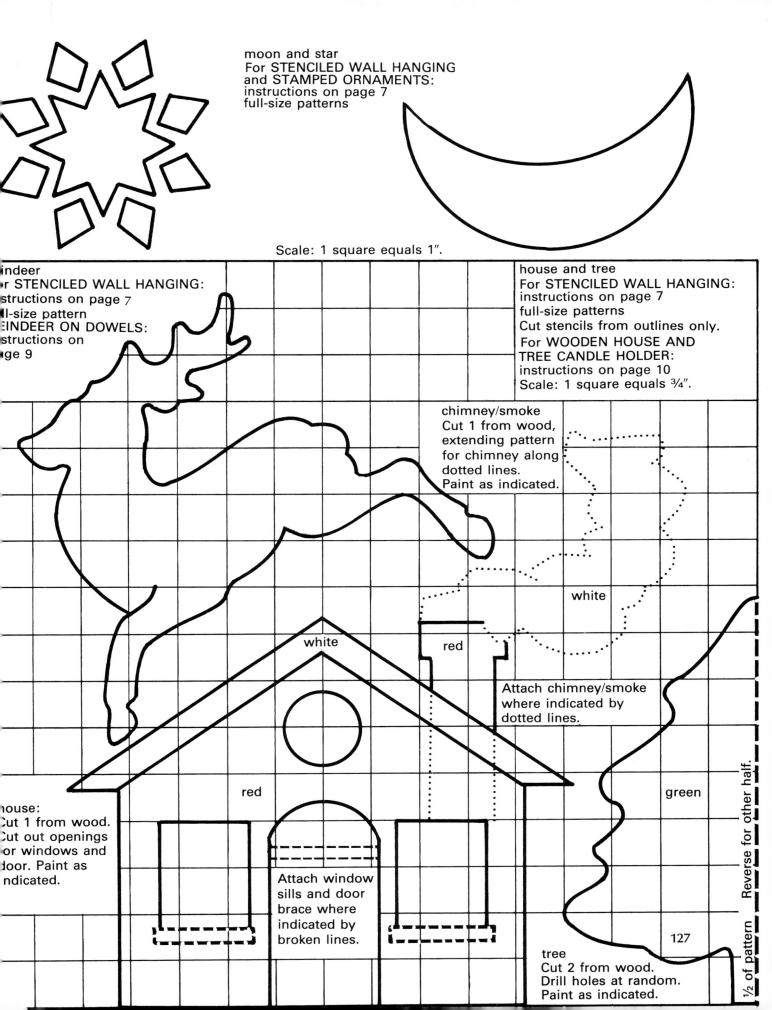

moon and star
For STENCILED WALL HANGING
and STAMPED ORNAMENTS:
instructions on page 7
full-size patterns

Scale: 1 square equals 1".

indeer
r STENCILED WALL HANGING:
structions on page 7
l-size pattern
EINDEER ON DOWELS:
structions on
ge 9

house and tree
For STENCILED WALL HANGING:
instructions on page 7
full-size patterns
Cut stencils from outlines only.
For WOODEN HOUSE AND
TREE CANDLE HOLDER:
instructions on page 10
Scale: 1 square equals ¾".

chimney/smoke
Cut 1 from wood,
extending pattern
for chimney along
dotted lines.
Paint as indicated.

white

white

red

Attach chimney/smoke
where indicated by
dotted lines.

red

green

ouse:
ut 1 from wood.
ut out openings
r windows and
oor. Paint as
ndicated.

Attach window
sills and door
brace where
indicated by
broken lines.

127

tree
Cut 2 from wood.
Drill holes at random.
Paint as indicated.

½ of pattern   Reverse for other half.

COUNTRY PINES QUILT

instructions on page 16
full-size pattern

Place on fold. →

Place on diagonal fold.

128

WEAVE SOME CHRISTMAS CHARM

instructions on page 44
full-size patterns

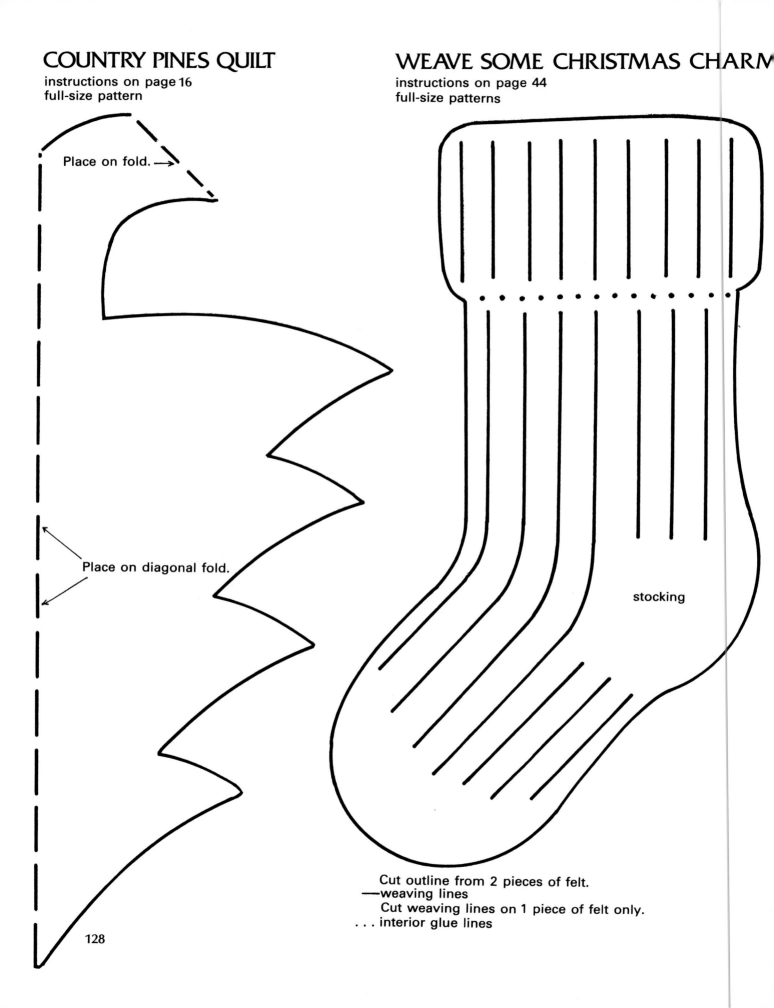

stocking

Cut outline from 2 pieces of felt.
—weaving lines
Cut weaving lines on 1 piece of felt only.
... interior glue lines

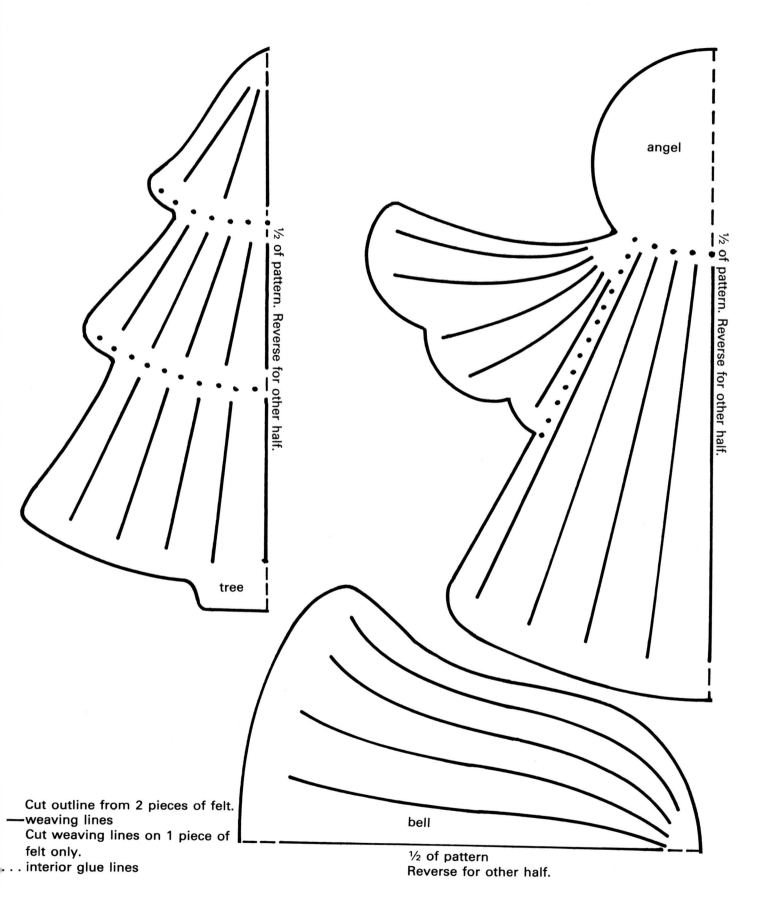

½ of pattern. Reverse for other half.

½ of pattern. Reverse for other half.

tree

angel

bell

Cut outline from 2 pieces of felt.
—— weaving lines
Cut weaving lines on 1 piece of felt only.
. . . interior glue lines

½ of pattern
Reverse for other half.

129

A VERSATILE CHRISTMAS QUILT

instructions on page 60
full-size patterns

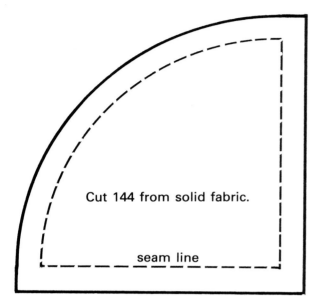

Cut 144 from solid fabric.

seam line

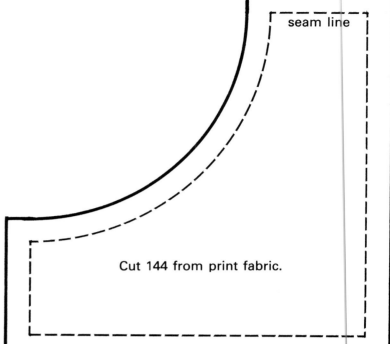

seam line

Cut 144 from print fabric.

A TRIO OF WOODEN ELVES

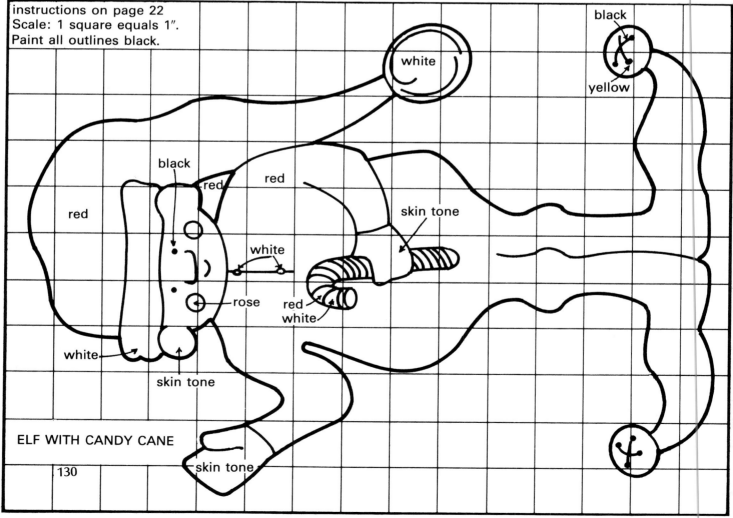

instructions on page 22
Scale: 1 square equals 1".
Paint all outlines black.

black

white

yellow

white

black

red

red

red

skin tone

black

white

rose

red
white

white

skin tone

ELF WITH CANDY CANE

130

skin tone

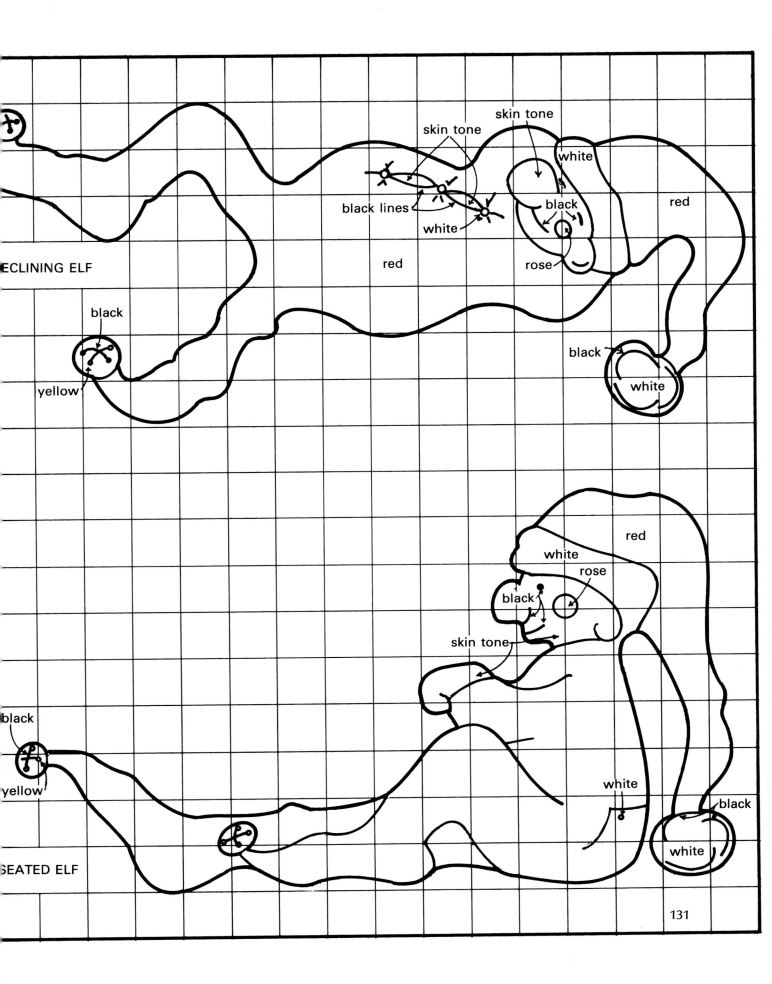

RECLINING ELF

SEATED ELF

131

STARS GALORE!
instructions on page 49
full-size patterns

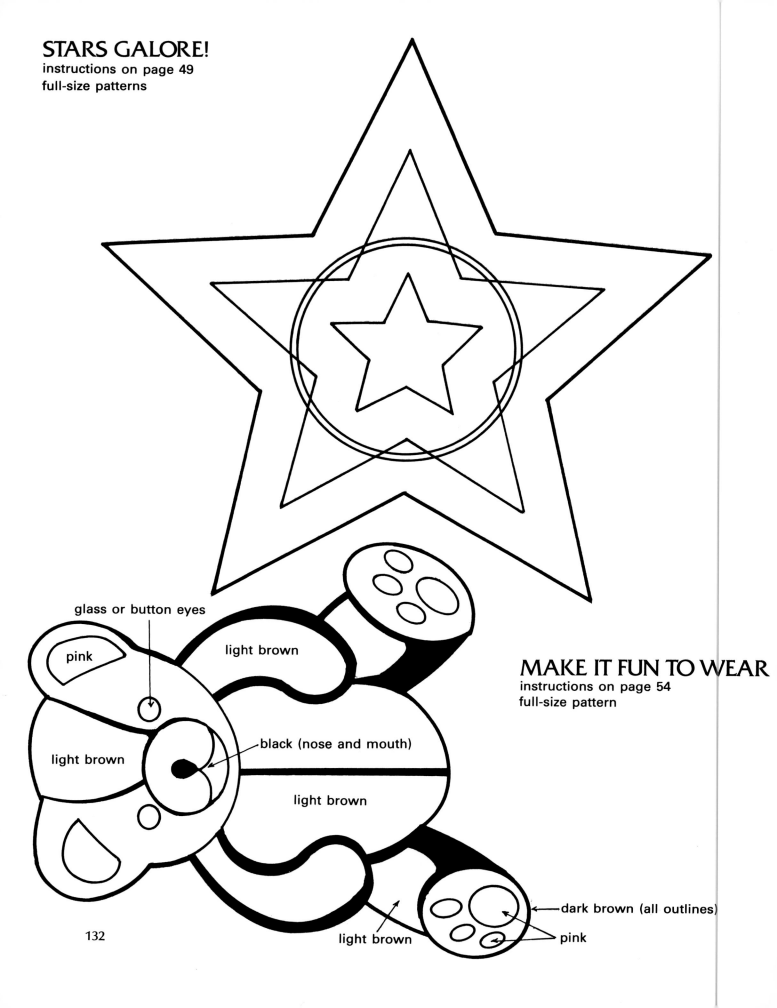

MAKE IT FUN TO WEAR
instructions on page 54
full-size pattern

glass or button eyes

pink

light brown

light brown

black (nose and mouth)

light brown

dark brown (all outlines)

light brown

pink

132

Color Key (DMC Flosses)	ANGEL WITH HORN ANGEL AND MOON		SNOWFLAKES

Color Key (DMC Flosses)

ANGEL WITH HORN / ANGEL AND MOON

- ◙ gold beads
- ⊠ 993 aqua
- ◪ 318 gray
- ◙ silver beads
- ◪ pink beads
- ⊡ 761 flesh
- ◪ 676 gold
- ◪ 943 aqua
- △ 321 red

- ◪ 613 beige
- ◩ yellow beads
- ◕ 435 brown
- ⊻ 762 gray
- ◩ 519 blue
- ■ 517 blue

Backstitch in black
to outline solid areas.

SNOWFLAKES

- ⊠ white
- ⊡ beads (colors desired)

Backstitch in silver metallic
to outline white areas.

133

SILHOUETTE THE SEASON

instructions on page 42
Scale: 1 square equals 2".

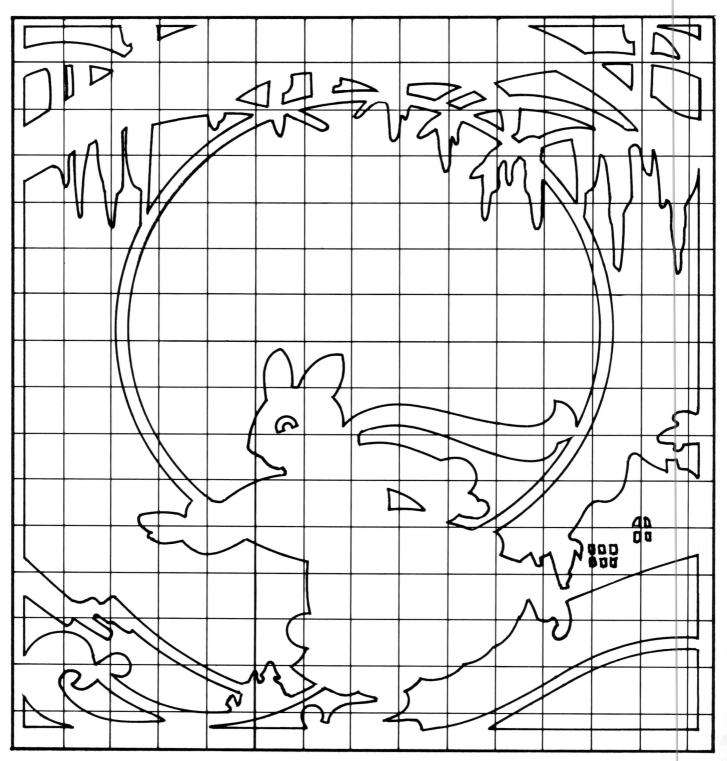

QUIET ELEGANCE FOR THE HOLIDAYS

Moiré and lace tree skirt
Instructions on page 30
Scale: 1 square equals 1".

fold line

skirt cutting line

rose scallop appliqué—
Cut 8.

fold line

rose scallop inset
Cut 7.

4B

5A

5B

2A

5C

5B

6C

3B

3B

4B

3B

3B

4A

3B

3B

2A

6B

1,2,3 D

5B

3A

3A

6B

5B

2B

4A

ACCENTS OF LACE AND EMBROIDERY

Embroidered lace fan
Instructions on page 34
Full-size pattern

Color Key
(DMC Flosses)
1—315 wine
2—316 mauve
3—778 pale mauve

4—3042 lavender
5—503 gray-green
6—504 light gray-green

Stitch Key
A—French knot
B—satin stitch
C—backstitch
D—bullion knot

NOTEWORTHY NOTEPADS

instructions on page 66
full-size patterns

leaf

leaf

tree

leaf

Machine-stitch along all lines.

136

A CHORUS OF CAROLERS

instructions on page 78
full-size patterns

Paint back red.

Paint sides same color as adjacent area on front.

137

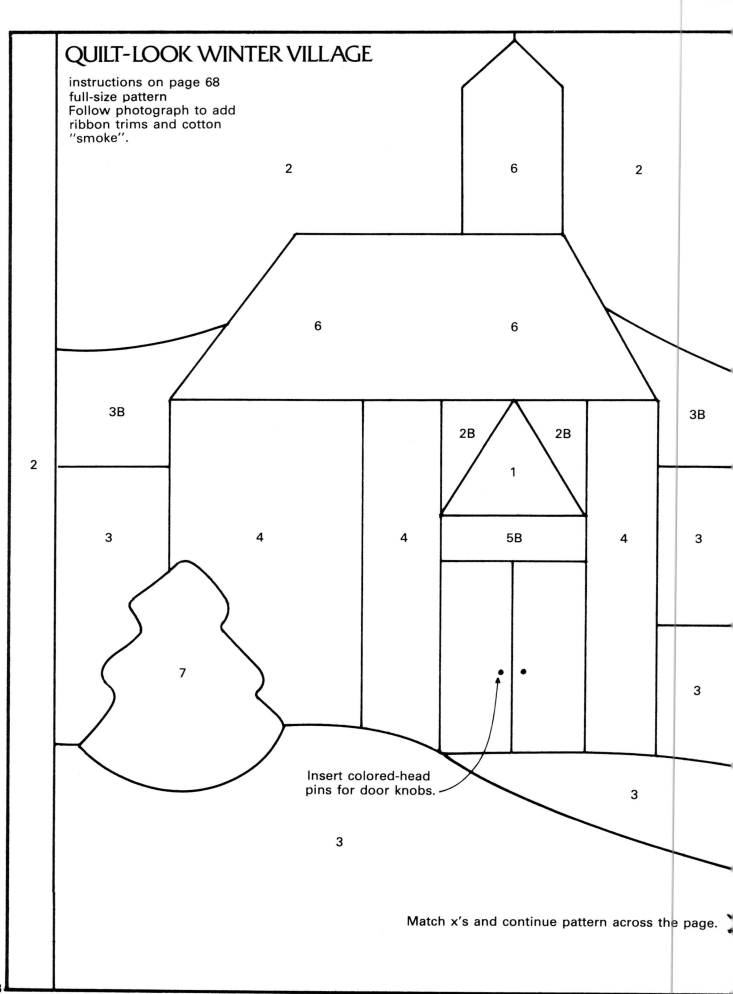

QUILT-LOOK WINTER VILLAGE

instructions on page 68
full-size pattern
Follow photograph to add
ribbon trims and cotton
"smoke".

2

6

2

6

6

6

3B

3B

2B

2B

1

2

3B

3B

3

4

4

4

3

5B

3

7

3

Insert colored-head
pins for door knobs.

3

3

3

Match x's and continue pattern across the page.

138

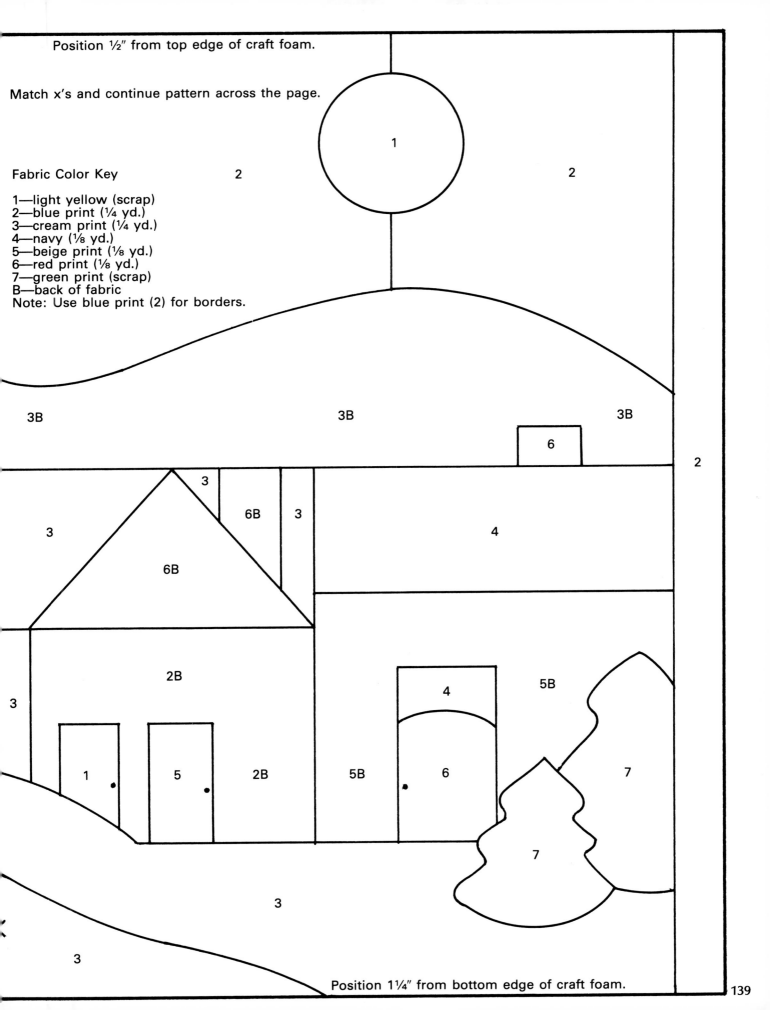

Position ½″ from top edge of craft foam.

Match x's and continue pattern across the page.

Fabric Color Key

1—light yellow (scrap)
2—blue print (¼ yd.)
3—cream print (¼ yd.)
4—navy (⅛ yd.)
5—beige print (⅛ yd.)
6—red print (⅛ yd.)
7—green print (scrap)
B—back of fabric
Note: Use blue print (2) for borders.

1

2

2

3B 3B 3B

6

2

3

3

6B 3

6B

4

3

2B

5B

3

1 5 2B 5B 4 6 7

7

3

3

Position 1¼″ from bottom edge of craft foam.

A PLAYFUL PUPPY PILLOW

instructions on page 70
full-size patterns
Add ¼″ seam allowance to all pattern pieces.

top of pillow

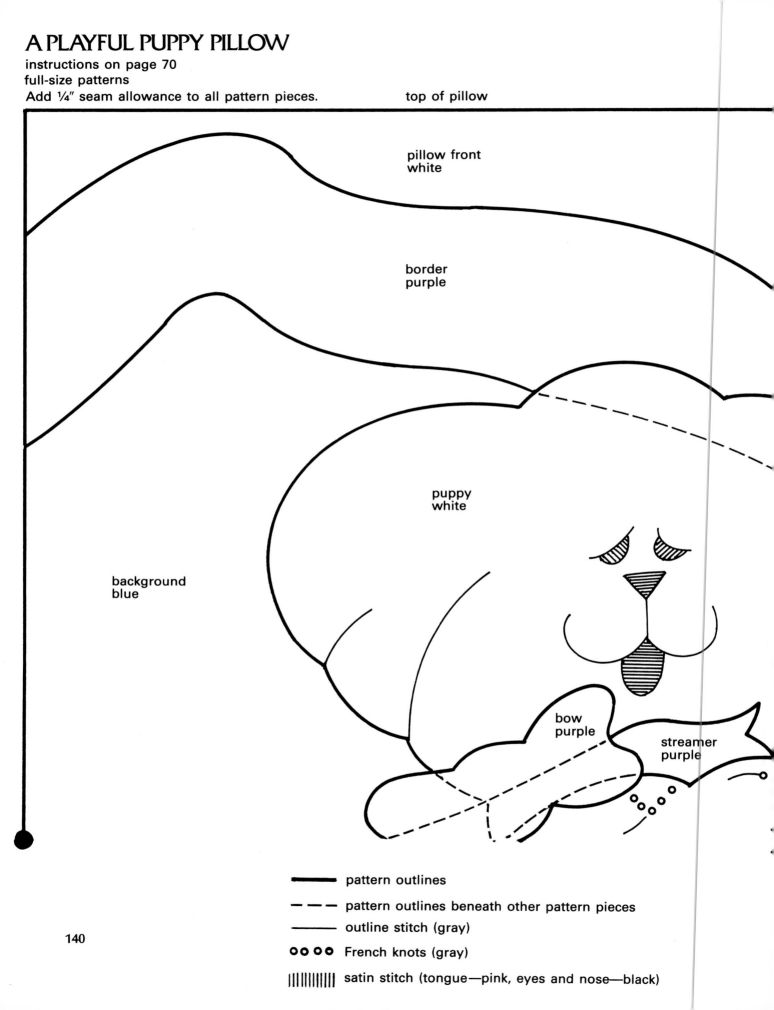

pillow front
white

border
purple

puppy
white

background
blue

bow
purple

streamer
purple

pattern outlines

pattern outlines beneath other pattern pieces

outline stitch (gray)

oo oo French knots (gray)

|||||||||| satin stitch (tongue—pink, eyes and nose—black)

140

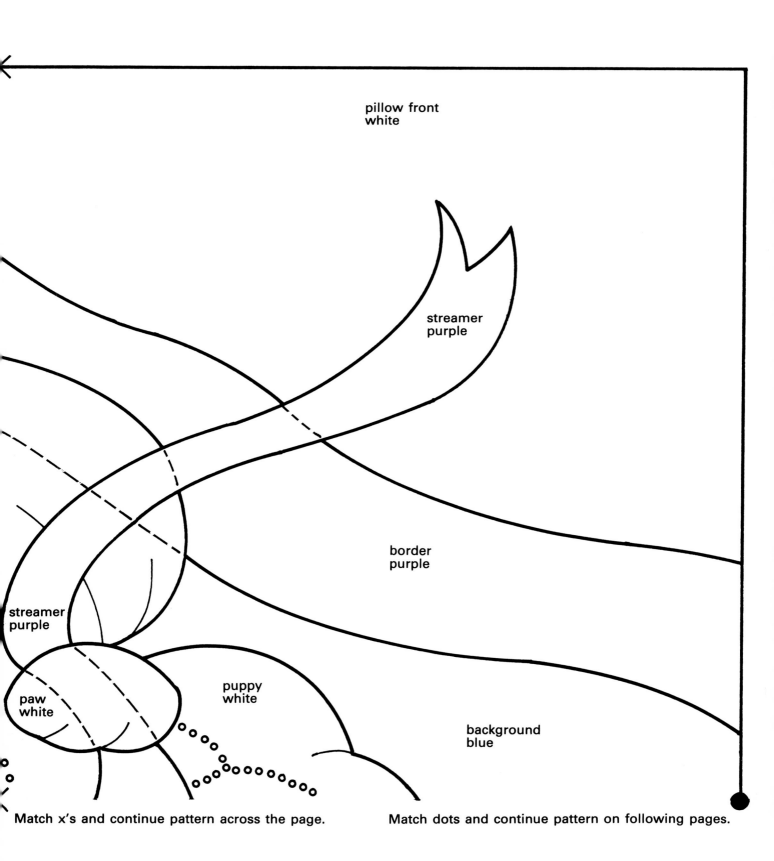

pillow front
white

streamer
purple

border
purple

streamer
purple

puppy
white

paw
white

background
blue

Match x's and continue pattern across the page.

Match dots and continue pattern on following pages.

141

A PLAYFUL PUPPY PILLOW

instructions on page 70
full-size patterns
Add ¼" seam allowance to all pattern pieces.

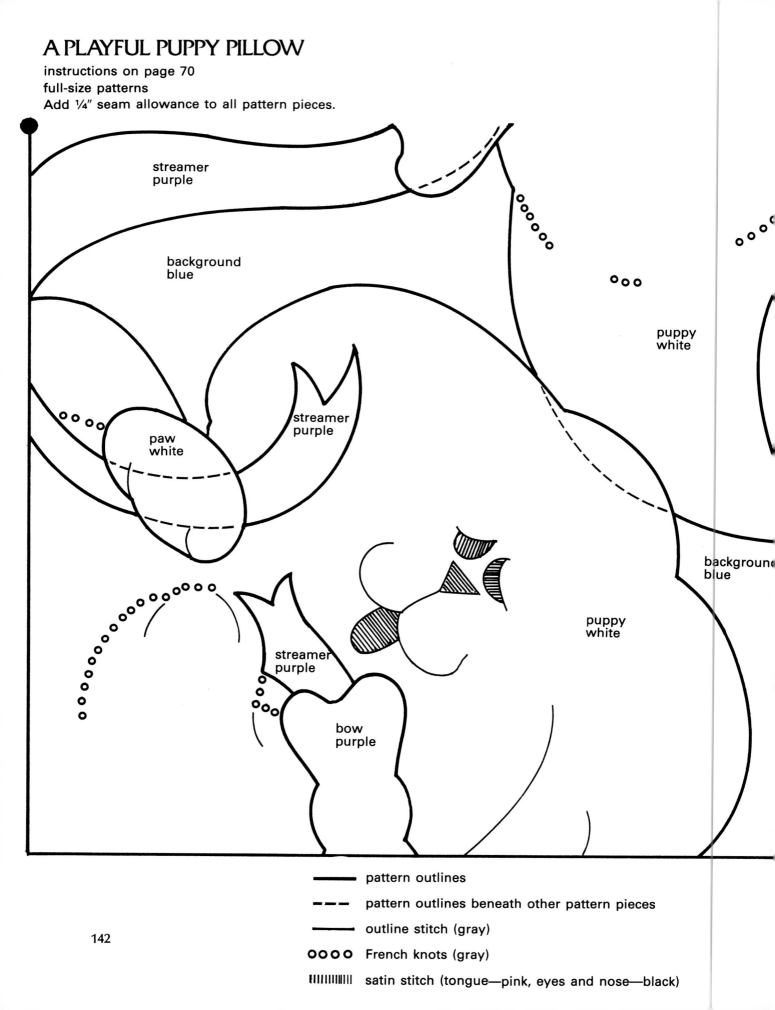

streamer
purple

background
blue

puppy
white

paw
white

streamer
purple

background
blue

puppy
white

streamer
purple

bow
purple

—————— pattern outlines

- - - - - pattern outlines beneath other pattern pieces

—————— outline stitch (gray)

OOOO French knots (gray)

IIIIIIIIIIIII satin stitch (tongue—pink, eyes and nose—black)

142

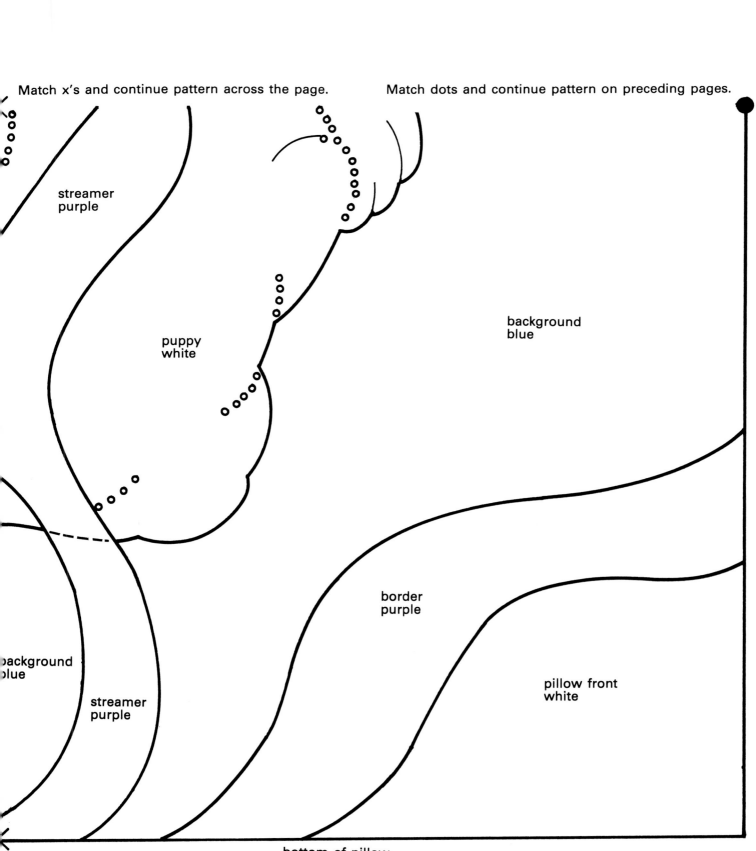

Match x's and continue pattern across the page. Match dots and continue pattern on preceding pages.

streamer
purple

puppy
white

background
blue

background
blue

streamer
purple

border
purple

pillow front
white

bottom of pillow

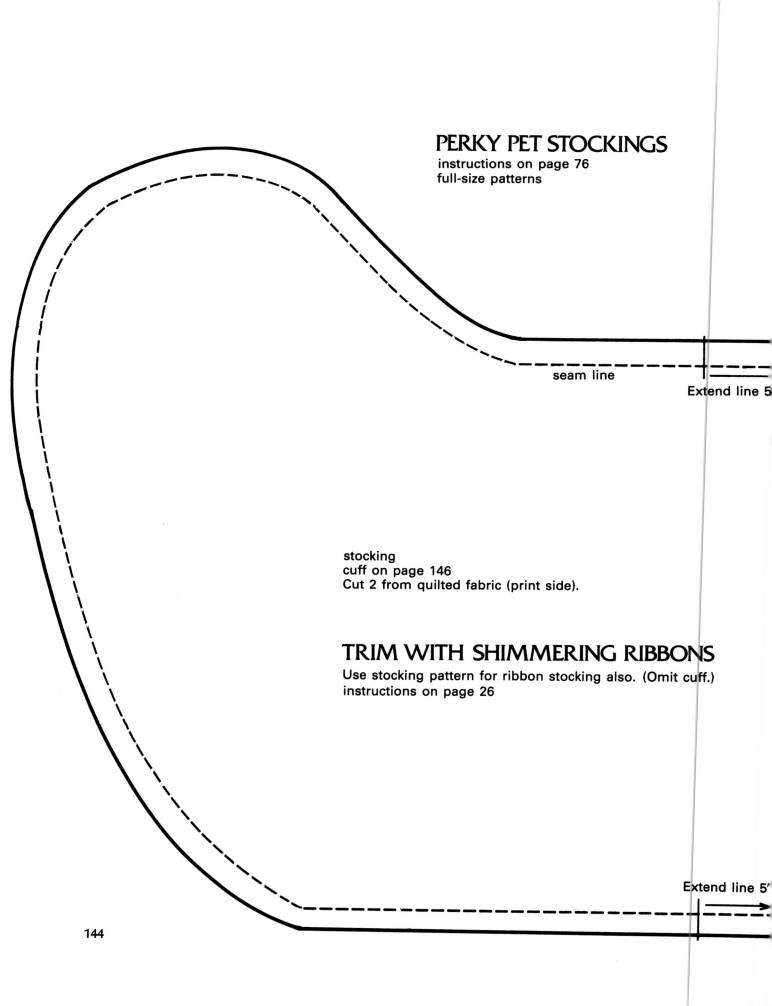

PERKY PET STOCKINGS

instructions on page 76
full-size patterns

seam line

Extend line 5

stocking
cuff on page 146
Cut 2 from quilted fabric (print side).

TRIM WITH SHIMMERING RIBBONS

Use stocking pattern for ribbon stocking also. (Omit cuff.)
instructions on page 26

Extend line 5"

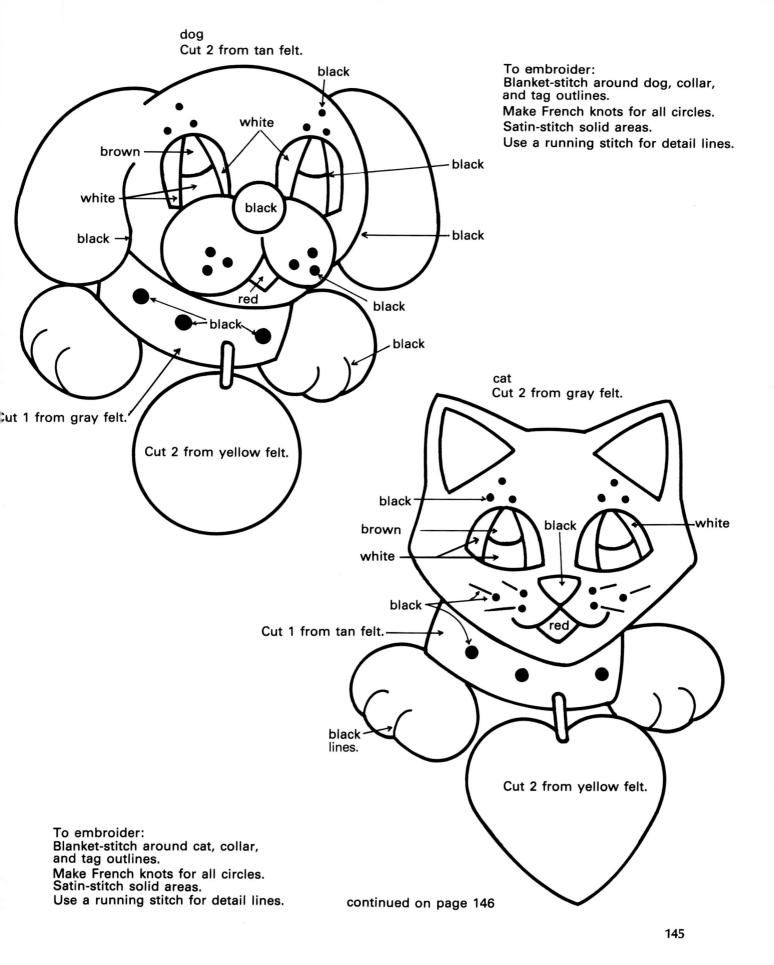

dog
Cut 2 from tan felt.

black

white

brown

white

black

black

black

black

black

black

red

black

black

Cut 1 from gray felt.

Cut 2 from yellow felt.

To embroider:
Blanket-stitch around dog, collar,
and tag outlines.
Make French knots for all circles.
Satin-stitch solid areas.
Use a running stitch for detail lines.

cat
Cut 2 from gray felt.

black

brown

white

black

white

black

red

Cut 1 from tan felt.

black
lines.

Cut 2 from yellow felt.

To embroider:
Blanket-stitch around cat, collar,
and tag outlines.
Make French knots for all circles.
Satin-stitch solid areas.
Use a running stitch for detail lines.

continued on page 146

PERKY PET STOCKINGS continued

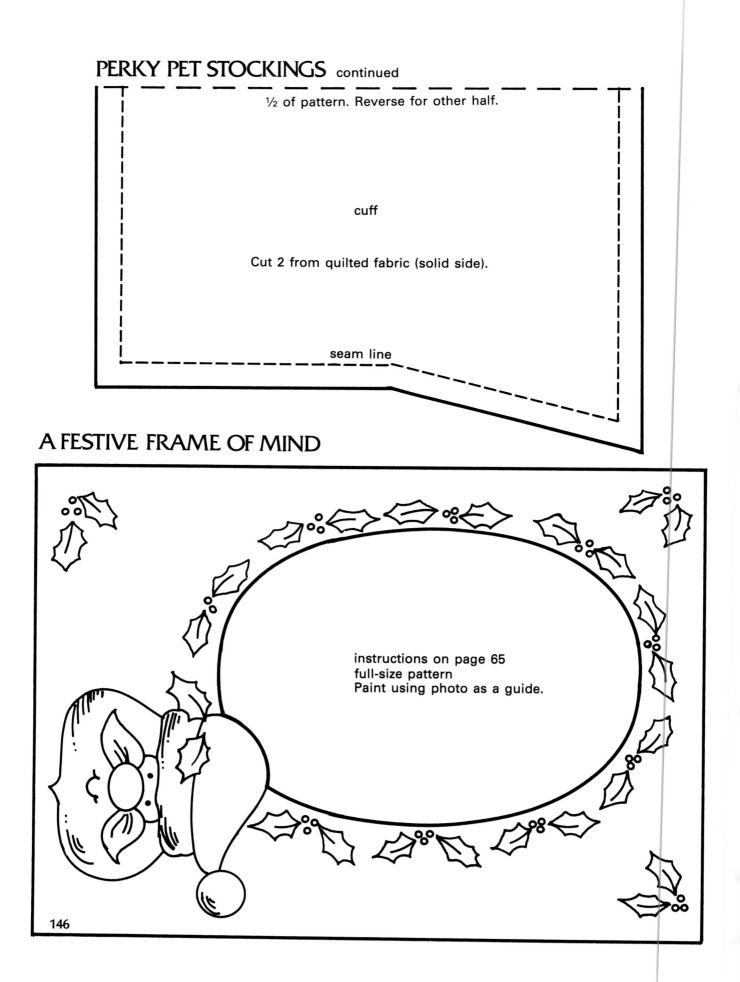

½ of pattern. Reverse for other half.

cuff

Cut 2 from quilted fabric (solid side).

seam line

A FESTIVE FRAME OF MIND

instructions on page 65
full-size pattern
Paint using photo as a guide.

PRESENT A PRETTY PAIR

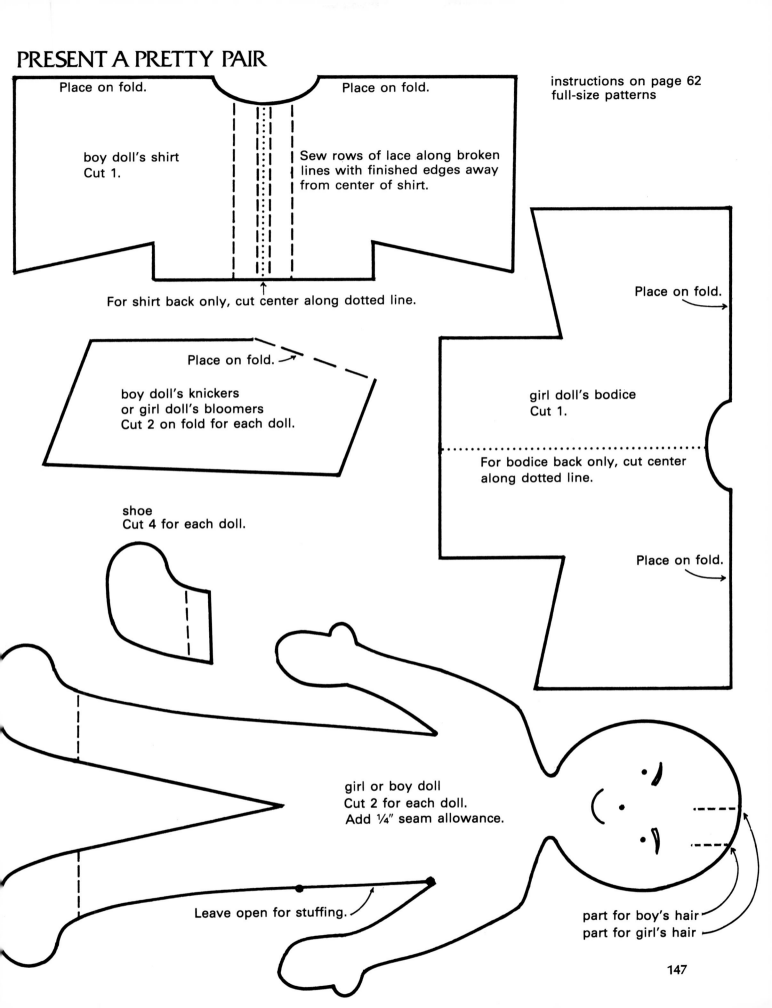

instructions on page 62
full-size patterns

Place on fold.

Place on fold.

boy doll's shirt
Cut 1.

Sew rows of lace along broken lines with finished edges away from center of shirt.

For shirt back only, cut center along dotted line.

Place on fold.

boy doll's knickers
or girl doll's bloomers
Cut 2 on fold for each doll.

Place on fold.

girl doll's bodice
Cut 1.

For bodice back only, cut center along dotted line.

Place on fold.

shoe
Cut 4 for each doll.

girl or boy doll
Cut 2 for each doll.
Add ¼" seam allowance.

Leave open for stuffing.

part for boy's hair
part for girl's hair

147

QUIET ELEGANCE FOR THE HOLIDAYS

diamond lace ornaments
instructions on page 32
full-size pattern

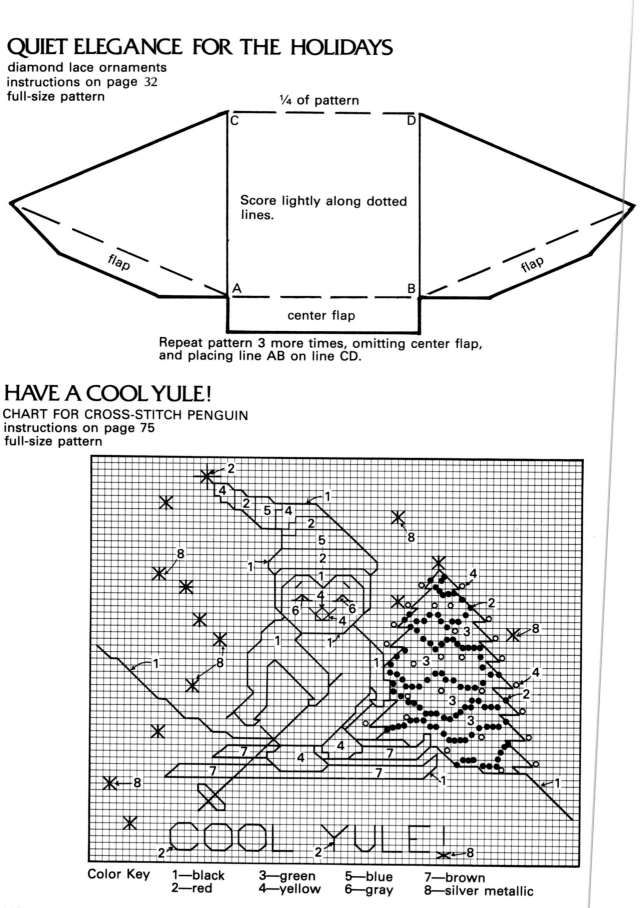

¼ of pattern

C   D

Score lightly along dotted lines.

flap

A   B

flap

center flap

Repeat pattern 3 more times, omitting center flap,
and placing line AB on line CD.

HAVE A COOL YULE!

CHART FOR CROSS-STITCH PENGUIN
instructions on page 75
full-size pattern

Color Key   1—black   3—green   5—blue   7—brown
                2—red   4—yellow   6—gray   8—silver metallic

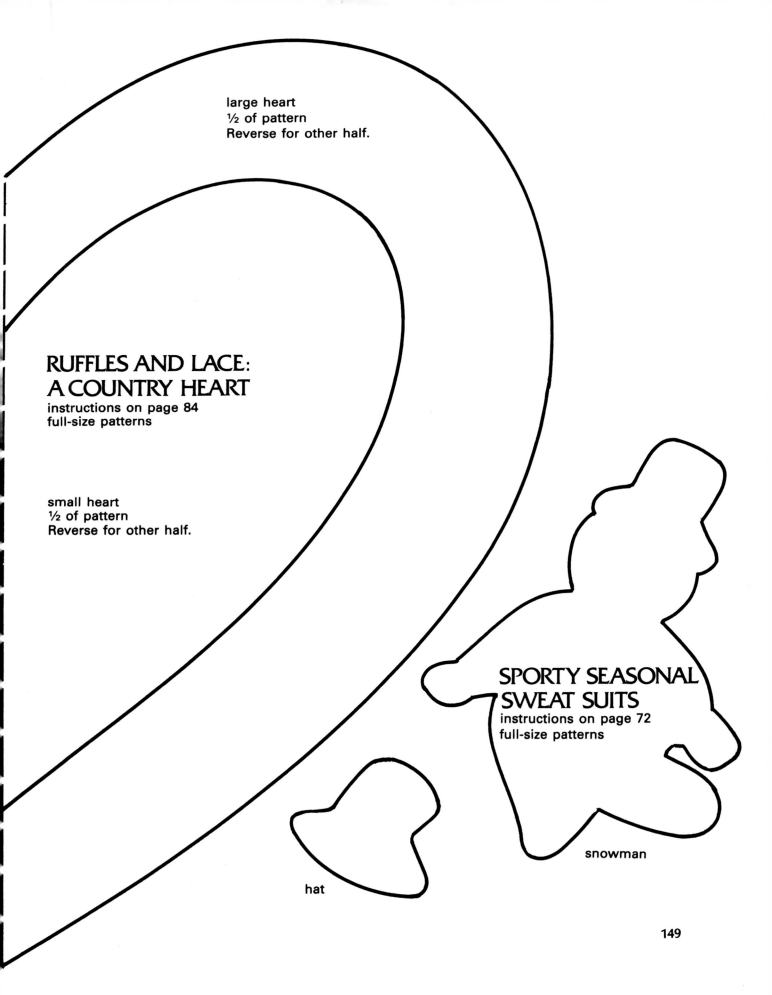

large heart
½ of pattern
Reverse for other half.

RUFFLES AND LACE:
A COUNTRY HEART
instructions on page 84
full-size patterns

small heart
½ of pattern
Reverse for other half.

SPORTY SEASONAL
SWEAT SUITS
instructions on page 72
full-size patterns

snowman

hat

MR. CLOWN MAKES IT ALL BETTER

instructions on page 80
full-size patterns

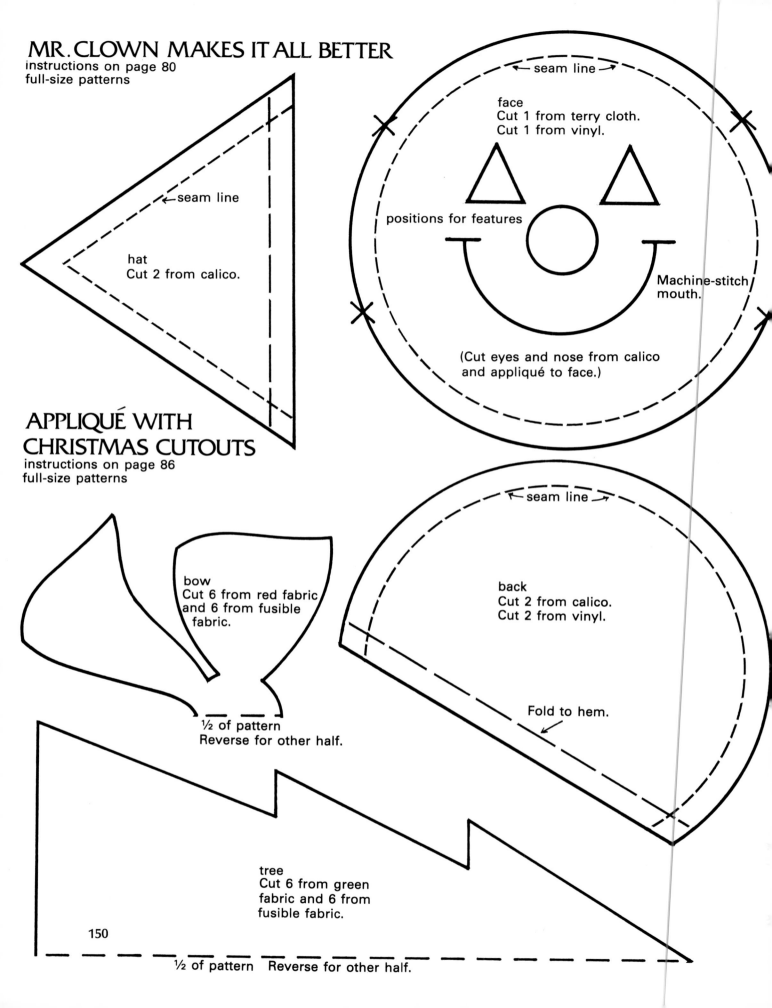

seam line

← seam line

hat
Cut 2 from calico.

face
Cut 1 from terry cloth.
Cut 1 from vinyl.

positions for features

Machine-stitch
mouth.

(Cut eyes and nose from calico
and appliqué to face.)

APPLIQUÉ WITH
CHRISTMAS CUTOUTS

instructions on page 86
full-size patterns

bow
Cut 6 from red fabric
and 6 from fusible
fabric.

← seam line →

back
Cut 2 from calico.
Cut 2 from vinyl.

Fold to hem.

½ of pattern
Reverse for other half.

tree
Cut 6 from green
fabric and 6 from
fusible fabric.

150

½ of pattern   Reverse for other half.

AN ANGEL OF AN APRON
instructions on page 90

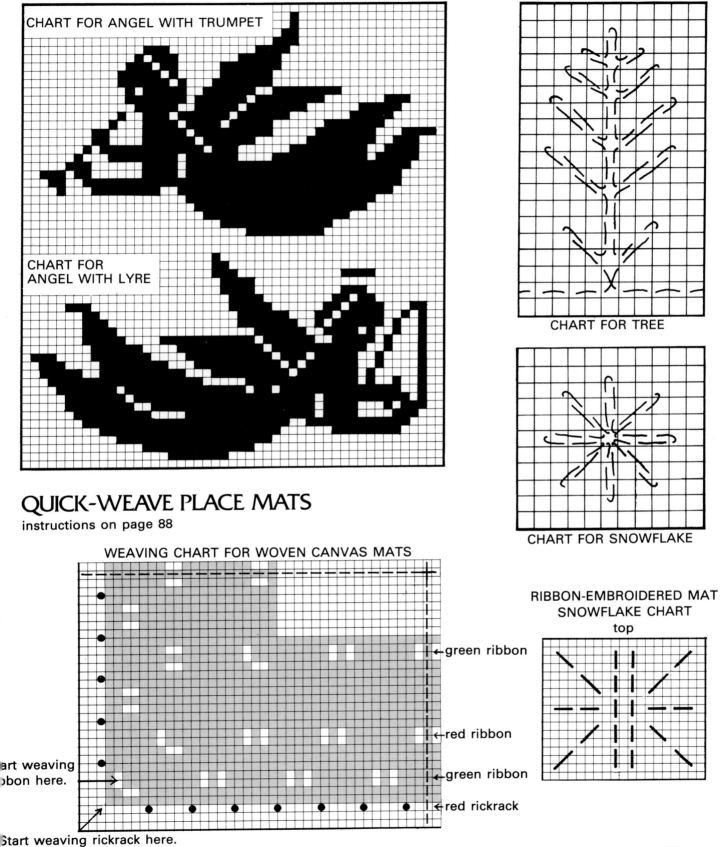

CHART FOR ANGEL WITH TRUMPET

CHART FOR
ANGEL WITH LYRE

QUICK-WEAVE PLACE MATS
instructions on page 88

WEAVING CHART FOR WOVEN CANVAS MATS

←green ribbon

←red ribbon

←green ribbon

←red rickrack

Start weaving
ribbon here.

Start weaving rickrack here.

CHART FOR TREE

CHART FOR SNOWFLAKE

RIBBON-EMBROIDERED MAT
SNOWFLAKE CHART
top

CONTRIBUTORS

Special thanks to Katherine Pearson, Editor of *Creative Ideas for Living*, for sharing concepts and materials, and to Charlotte Hagood, Needlecrafts Editor of *Creative Ideas for Living*, for providing technical assistance with needlecrafts. Thanks also to the *Southern Living* Test Kitchens staff for preparing recipes.

DESIGNERS:

PHOTOGRAPHERS: